Making the Church
Our Own

Making the Church Our Own

How We Can Reform the Catholic Church from the Ground Up

Leonard Swidler

A SHEED & WARD BOOK

ROWMAN & LITTLEFIELD PUBLISHERS, INC.
Lanham • Boulder • New York • Toronto • Plymouth, UK

A SHEED & WARD BOOK

ROWMAN & LITTLEFIELD PUBLISHERS, INC.

Published in the United States of America
by Rowman & Littlefield Publishers, Inc.
A wholly owned subsidiary of The Rowman & Littlefield Publishing Group, Inc.
4501 Forbes Boulevard, Suite 200, Lanham, Maryland 20706
www.rowmanlittlefield.com

Estover Road
Plymouth PL6 7PY
United Kingdom

British Library Cataloguing in Publication Information Available

Library of Congress Cataloging-in-Publication Data

Swidler, Leonard J.
  Making the church our own : how we can reform the Catholic Church from the
ground up / Leonard Swidler.
      p. cm.
  "A Sheed & Ward book."
  Includes bibliographical references and index.
  ISBN-13: 978-1-58051-215-2 (pbk. : alk. paper)
  ISBN-10: 1-58051-215-1 (pbk. : alk. paper)
  1. Catholic Church—Government. 2. Church renewal—Catholic Church. I.
Title.
  BX1803.S95 2007
  262'.02—dc22

                                    2006101840

Printed in the United States of America

♾™ The paper used in this publication meets the minimum requirements of
American National Standard for Information Sciences—Permanence of Paper for
Printed Library Materials, ANSI/NISO Z39.48–1992.

Contents

The Argument

$\mathcal{T}$he gist of my argument is this: Because the Catholic Church has been for centuries, and still is today, the largest and most powerful institution of religious and moral influence in the world, it is vital for human welfare to reform it so that it will provide the strong moral and spiritual leadership—in concert with others—that the world desperately needs. However, an effective reform, though it must penetrate deeply to the interior spiritual and ethical core, absolutely must also secure those interior and exterior reforms *in law*! Otherwise they will in a few short decades, or sooner, be washed away in the historical tides of change that are always sweeping over humankind.

The rock-solid evidence for this argument is found in the comparison of the extraordinarily profound reforms of Catholicism that were initiated in Vatican Council II (1962–65) and those of a strikingly similar sort by the *Enlightenment* Catholicism of a significant part of Germany during the first third of the nineteenth century, "which were all swept away in the historical tides of change"— because they were not secured in the canon law and practice of the Catholic Church on the highest levels.

After presenting the evidence in some detail—the similarities are really quite stunning!—I will offer my suggestions on how to learn from this lesson of history, and not repeat its sad past.

These suggestions include, primarily, casting all the necessary reforms—e.g., accountability, transparency, shared decision making, representativeness, due process of law, and shared property ownership —foundationally in the legal instrument of the Parish (and eventually Diocesan, National, and ultimately Global) Constitutions. These Constitutions, besides being legally registered, need also to be formally installed liturgically and annually renewed. The world needs "Constitutional Catholicism"!

I

ENLIGHTENMENT CATHOLICISM

· 1 ·

What Is Enlightenment Catholicism?

$\mathcal{H}$istorians of the West often speak of modern times starting around the beginning of the sixteenth century, with the discovery by Europeans of the "New World" in 1492, and the splintering of Christian unity in the West with the beginning of the Protestant Reformation, launched in 1517 when Martin Luther nailed his ninety-five theses to the church door in Wittenberg. German scholars speak of *die Neuzeit* (the New Time) beginning in the eighteenth century. The English term would probably be *modernity*. This period is perhaps best known as the "Age of Reason," or even more so as the Enlightenment.

The word *Enlightenment* in the English-speaking Catholic world, or *Aufklärung* in the German-speaking Catholic world, has since the middle of the nineteenth century almost always had a derogatory connotation. The histories of the Catholic Church in Germany in the nineteenth century have usually depicted the Enlightenment as a cesspool of vice and have either denigrated or ignored the efforts of those German Catholics who worked for reforms inspired by the Enlightenment during the first half of the nineteenth century. Even such a highly reputed Catholic historian as Franz Schnabel, writing in the 1930s, tended only to grant that Enlightenment Catholicism did contribute a few things to the welfare of the Church and was not so entirely black as it had been painted; but he insisted on the whole there was clearly more mischief than

3

good there.[1] Enlightenment Catholicism was often pictured as rationalistic in the reductionist deist sense, as if it emphasized reason to the point of eliminating revelation. It was described as if it wished to destroy the institutional church, undermine all theology, corrupt morals, and strip the liturgy of all meaning.

While it may be true to say these things of some thinkers, activists, and perhaps even churchmen, particularly in France, they are gross distortions—in fact, countersigns—of the reality of most Enlightenment Catholicism in Germany. Enlightenment Catholicism was a reform Catholicism, and a reform movement, regardless of what those in power think at the time, is not out to destroy an institution, but rather to re-form it. True, it may not be in a manner that is to the liking of those in power, probably because they would lose some of their personal power. But this is radically different from a movement which sets out to destroy an institution, as, for example, Communism attempted to destroy institutional religion.

In the background of Enlightenment Catholicism there were several movements which grew out of the Enlightenment, but were really apart from it, even predecessors to it in certain areas. They were "Gallicanism," "Febronianism," and "Josephinism." Let me describe them in the briefest fashion.

Gallicanism is a doctrine that grew up in France (previously known as Gaul; hence the name Gallican) starting in the thirteenth century as taught at the Sorbonne (founded 1257). It developed further during the fourteenth- to fifteenth-century "Western Schism" when there were two or three popes simultaneously, and still more in the wake of the sixteenth-century Protestant Reformation. The basic teaching was that the decrees of Rome could take effect in France only with the appropriate French approvals. One version was "Royal Gallicanism" wherein the king had the right of (dis)approval; a second was "Episcopal Gallicanism" wherein the Assembly of French bishops had the right of (dis)approval; and the third was "Parliamentarian Gallicanism" wherein the French Parliament had the right of (dis)approval. Gallicanism was dominant in France until after the Napoleonic period (ended 1815).

Febronianism in many ways was a mid-eighteenth-century German counterpart of Gallicanism. The three Archbishop Electors of the Emperor of the Holy Roman Empire commissioned Bishop Nicholas von Hontheim of Trier to do an analysis of the German Church's grievances against Rome. The result was his essay published under the pen name Justinus Febronius. He advocated that as far as possible, German Church affairs should be kept in German episcopal and civil hands.

Josephinism receives its name from Emperor Joseph II of Austria (sole emperor 1780–90), who not only basically followed the principles of Gallicanism and Febronianism, but also was very active in reforming and restructuring the Catholic Church within his empire. He did so not only without waiting for permission from Rome but often in direct opposition to Rome. His aggressiveness in many ways put the Enlightenment (and reform) in a subsequently disadvantageous light.

In the area of theology, Enlightenment Catholicism tried to lift what it saw as the dead hand of authoritarian dogmatism by putting what it thought was a rational basis under it all—an action it felt helped to promote rather than undermine theology. That Enlightenment Catholicism advocated some positions in theology which were later modified or rejected by ecumenical councils is doubtless true; that its opposition, including the official Catholic Magisterium, as in Pope Gregory XVI's 1832 encyclical *Mirari vos*, also suffered the same fate is also absolutely certain. (Compare that encyclical with the "Declaration of Religious Freedom" of Vatican II—more about that below.) When the charge against Enlightenment Catholicism of the corruption of morals is looked into a little further, it turns out that it was being accused of the promotion of individual freedom and responsibility in things like religious liberty and freedom of speech. As for stripping the liturgy of form and meaning, as the charge against it was often made, Enlightenment Catholicism strove for, and often attained, the exact opposite. It wished to reform the liturgy to make it meaningful to the people.

A brief word must be said here about the use of the term *Enlightenment Catholicism* in these pages. Although English scholars are accustomed to using the term *Enlightenment* mainly in connection with the latter half of the eighteenth century, German scholars often find the reality of the Enlightenment running well into the first half of nineteenth-century German history, and hence they frequently use the term *Enlightenment* to refer to pertinent persons and elements throughout that half of the nineteenth century. Occasionally German scholars will refer to the Enlightenment in the nineteenth century as the Late Enlightenment (*Spät-Aufklärung*), but more often they simply say *Aufklärung*—Enlightenment. The same is also true of the term *Enlightenment Catholicism* since the movement for the reform of Catholicism "in the light of reason," broadly understood, did not reach its high point till the 1830s, and made one last desperate attempt to survive in 1848.[2]

One Catholic scholar noted that "The powerful movement of the Enlightenment, which in Germany was dominant throughout the entire eighteenth century and the first decades of the nineteenth century, did not stop in front of the Catholic Church."[3] Another wrote:

> Timewise the moderate Enlightenment period cannot be precisely fixed. In general it extends somewhat later than the extreme type, running far into the Romantic period [*in die Romantik*]. Its limitation must flow from the history of ideas. Still, some who came to the fore in their writing in the twenties and thirties of the nineteenth century belong in this period [*Aufklärung*]. These men . . . cannot be dismissed simply because they were called Enlightenment Catholics [*Aufklärer*].[4]

In fact, the polarity of positions held among German Catholic clergy regarding the Enlightenment at that time was well exemplified in a contemporary archconservative periodical where the anonymous author referred to the *Badischen Kirchenblatt* as an "un-Catholic" and "unchurchly" paper, whereas the statement that author quoted from the Baden clergy began by praising the bishop of Rottenburg in southwest Germany, Johan Baptist von Keller, for promoting an authentic "Enlightenment" in his diocese in 1837.[5]

A more descriptive term for this movement for Catholic reform in late-eighteenth and early-nineteenth-century German Catholicism might be "Reform Catholicism." But in fact German scholars use that term, *Reformkatholizismus*, for the movement of Catholic reform at the end of the nineteenth century and refer to the earlier movement simply as the Enlightenment in Catholicism.[6]

When one digs through the often anonymous defamation of Enlightenment Catholicism, a picture emerges that is extraordinarily similar to the Catholicism that arose over a century later from Vatican Council II (1962–65). But this latter Catholicism developed without any overt continuity with the former, which was reviled in its day by those who eventually triumphed over it. Even the memory of Enlightenment Catholicism and the reputations of its advocates have for the most part been obliterated, or, where that was not possible or desirable, distorted beyond all recognition by Catholic historians—and they were almost the only ones to write on the subject.

Although it is the first task of the historian to attempt to describe her/his subject as objectively as possible, *"wie es eigentlich gewesen ist"* (as it really was), analyzing and evaluating its various elements within its own context, such a properly executed task is by no means bereft of subjectivity. The very decision to undertake a specific task arises from within the historian as some kind of response to his/her contemporary context. My historical study here was prompted by noticing how many of the positions approved and advocated at Vatican II seemed to resemble condemned positions attributed (albeit in very truncated fashion) to German Catholics of the first half of the nineteenth century. This observation naturally gave rise to the question of what this earlier Catholicism really was like—as seen in the primary documents rather than through the filter of its enemies' descriptions—and secondarily how much it really was or was not like Vatican II Catholicism.

Research in the libraries of southwestern Germany has proved extremely revealing. It is clear that a non-tendentious history of the entirety of Enlightenment Catholicism awaits writing. It is partly as a step on the way toward the fulfilling of that task that these pages are written. For example, a very obvious area of great similarity between Enlightenment Catholicism and Vatican II reform is that of liturgical reform. Noticing this similarity was intensified by the at times almost feverish concern of mid-twentieth-century Catholic advocates of liturgical reform to disassociate themselves from the liturgical-reform efforts of the early nineteenth century, of Enlightenment Catholicism.[7] One immediately wondered if the gentlemen do protest too much.

If the reforms of Enlightenment and Vatican II Catholicism are found to be substantially similar—which is the hypothesis here—the implications will be manifold, not only for Catholic scholarship and life, but also for the scholarship and life of those non-Catholics who come into significant contact with the Catholic Church, the largest Christian body in the world—around 1.2 billion members in the twenty-first century.

One implication such a result would have for Catholic scholarship would be a further discrediting of that powerful authoritarian mentality that dominated Roman Catholicism for many generations until Vatican II, and has been striving to make a comeback in the last third of a century. The Catholic Church in its authoritative structures does at times make what it later in practice recognizes as errors; basic commitments are made which are later reversed. Having historical documentation of such relativizes the old authoritarian claims. One implication such a result would have for non-Catholic scholarship would be to force it to take a more cautious, at times even skeptical, attitude toward descriptions of the "only acceptable" Catholic positions on various issues, because the Catholic Church does reverse itself officially on basic issues—despite the most emphatic protestations to the contrary.

Perhaps one of the most basic constitutive elements of the historical setting at the beginning of the nineteenth century lies over a century back, namely, the Scientific Revolution of the seventeenth century. The previous work of Copernicus, Kepler, Galileo, and others found in a way a synthesis and culmination in the world-forming work of Sir Isaac Newton (1642–1727). As a result of Newton's work, and that of many other scientists, though supremely his, the world was seen as something eminently *rational*. And because the world was rational in all of its parts, all men and women needed to do to understand it was to study it diligently. They did not need to assume that they would never be able to solve the riddles of the universe; in fact, they should assume the opposite—look at Newton! Because the universe was essentially rational and because men and women were essentially rational, they had every hope and expectation of understanding the world. Then, once they understood it, they would be in a position to form and shape it in a manner that would most perfectly fulfill the world and, at the same time, naturally, be most beneficial to humanity—again, because both were essentially rational. Eighteenth-century men and women, moreover, did not feel they came to this new, self-confident, optimistic worldview by some sort of leap of faith, for the Newtonian *Weltanschauung* of a rational universe was constantly proved anew and extended even by dozens and scores of amateur scientists, throughout the eighteenth century; Benjamin Franklin and Thomas Jefferson are two famous examples in our own American history.

Doubtless just as basic a constitutive element of the historical setting of the beginning of the nineteenth century was the dynamic development in the economic sphere: the Commercial and Industrial Revolutions. One does not need to be a Marxist to recognize the basic force of economics in history, although it was largely thanks to Karl Marx that the fundamental quality of this aspect of humanity's life was somewhat more properly focused on. For a long time in Western civilization the dominant class was the aristocracy, lay and clerical, because they were the landholders, and land was the only really major source of wealth and power. However, the long development of the middle class, from the medieval growth of towns, the burgeoning of trade in the Renaissance, and fantastic trade expansion in the Age of Discovery and Colonialism, took an even greater leap forward with the coming of the Industrial Revolution, which began in England in the middle of the eighteenth century. As a result of the Commercial and Industrial Revolutions, the middle class was called into existence and, by the latter part of the eighteenth century, was catapulted into a position of great influence and, as in the cases of the American and French Revolutions, even of dominance.

However, while the Industrial Revolution tended to lift the middle class into power, it also initiated the Age of the Masses. More and more peasants were drawn or driven from the land into the cities, or rather into the human swamps that formed around and in the cities. As business men and women and aristocrats with a business eye turned more and more land away from communal support to making an immediate monetary profit, more and more peasants could no longer exist in their ancestral villages. At the same time the same or similar business people were setting up factories in the cities which demanded manual laborers—cheap.

Where in a society based on the land each individual had his and her own proper place and function in relation to all others, in the society based on commerce and industry a growing number of individuals became a part of a mass, with no specific proper place or proper function. However, this growth of a mass proletariat took place at different times in different countries; England was first, starting in the latter part of the eighteenth century. This Age of the Masses developed in many directions, such as in the beginnings of mass education, mass communications through the spread of literacy and the cheap newspaper, ever more rapid transportation, and mass involvement in politics through the rise of democracy and socialism.

In the area of politics the dominance of the aristocracy was first curtailed or at least somewhat controlled by the monarchy, which became "absolute" in the sixteenth century, but which by the middle of the eighteenth century tended to be an "Enlightened Despotism." Here the new worldview of reason made itself felt, to some extent, through the Enlightened Prince, the modern version of Plato's Philosopher King. One thinks preeminently of Frederick the Great of Prussia, Catherine the Great of Russia, and Maria Theresa and Joseph II of Austria; but there were also many other "Enlightened Despots" of lesser fame in the latter part of the eighteenth century.

If *reason* was one key word that characterized the historical setting of the beginning of the nineteenth century, another key word was *freedom*. Freedom was sought in every sphere, and it was heralded as the prime promoter of humanity's welfare, along with reason, its essential counterpart. In economics the move was away from the state's control through the mercantilist system; in social and political affairs it was away from the dominance of aristocratic and royal privileges; in thought and religion it was toward freedom from the tyranny of a stultifying authority and deadening tradition.

These two ideas, reason and freedom, burst into flames in 1789 with the French Revolution. Reason as an instrument of the "Enlightened Despot" was no longer considered a sufficient advance; reason had to become the instrument of all free men and women. But reason and freedom in many ways ran amok during the Revolution; it ran into the tyranny of the Reign of Terror and later of the tyrant, Napoleon. Still, even under Napoleon, and in many ways because of his genius, many economic, social, political, and legal structures were "rationalized" and millions of men and women were liberated from a variety of oppressors. But the tyranny of France called forth, only very slowly at first, the resistance of an ever broader collection of men and women in the dominated lands. The form this resistance tended to take was that of nationalism.

Nationalism, as it developed in the nineteenth and twentieth centuries, was also a product of the Age of the Masses. It is hard to see how it could have developed in anything like the manner it did without an uprooted popular base, without mass education, communication, and transportation. Only with such building blocks could something beyond a provincial structure or a loyalty to a dynasty be erected. Nevertheless it was the French Revolution that fused all those elements, and others, into modern nationalism, first in France itself, and then, in reaction to France's tyranny, in Germany, Italy, and elsewhere.

One other major thing must be said about the general historical setting in Europe at the beginning of the nineteenth century: rationalism did not reign unchallenged; in fact, it called forth its antithesis, Romanticism. Where rationalism stressed reason, logic, clarity, and reform on those bases, Romanticism tended, among other things, to stress feeling, paradox, the mystical, and, in Germany at any rate, reaction. However, the rise of Romanticism was not like a light switch thrown on January 1, 1800. It had antecedents, particularly in Germany in the *Sturm und Drang* of the latter half of the eighteenth century, and the Enlightenment, the *Aufklärung*, continued to be a strong, though waning, force throughout much of the first half of the nineteenth century.

It is against this general European background that the reform efforts of the Catholics of the Enlightenment in Germany must be seen. In Germany itself, it must be recalled that there had been no unified state since the break-up of the empire of Charlemagne in the ninth century. There were actually hundreds of states in the Germanies at the beginning of the nineteenth century, which chaotic situation was changed by Napoleon during the first decade of that century; he reduced the number of states to a dozen or so, all subservient to him. This political change drastically affected the Catholic Church in Germany since there had been many ecclesiastical principalities— that is, states with archbishops, bishops, or abbots as chiefs of state. These ecclesiastical states were almost entirely eliminated as ecclesiastical states; the land was turned over to secular princes, who were then beholden to Napoleon. Also huge numbers of abbeys, convents, churches, etc., were secularized—that is, turned over to the state, which then sold or distributed them. But before the secularization took place there was a strong movement among German bishops to steer a course of relative independence vis-à-vis Rome, particularly exemplified, as noted, by the efforts of Bishop Johann Nicholaus von Hontheim, a.k.a. "Febronius," advocating greater episcopal power vis-à-vis Rome, much as the Gallicans were doing in France.

It should also be recalled that even in those German states which were not ecclesiastical principalities there was a tradition of union of church and state of one and a half millennias' standing. The official church ever since the fourth century had been in favor of this union, but always in the sense that the state would either be subservient to the church or at least would promote the welfare of the church as the official church understood that welfare, but certainly not in the sense that the state might undertake to reform the church. But it was exactly this latter effort that was made in the Austrian lands during the time of Maria Theresa (empress 1740–80) and most particularly her son Joseph II (sole emperor 1780–90). It had a profound effect not only in the Austrian lands but also elsewhere, since it was often imitated. It is in this area of church-state relations that we will find the most glaring difference between Enlightenment Catholicism and Vatican II Catholicism.

Obviously the Enlightenment Catholics of late eighteenth- and early nineteenth-century Germany were concerned about reform of the liturgy, though not only that, important as they thought that was. Their *Weltanschauung* mandated reform in practically every area of life, sacred and secular. Within the confines of these pages it is of course not possible to describe these reforms thoroughly, but I will nevertheless attempt to provide an outline of the major reform efforts of Enlightenment Catholics, starting with liturgical reform.

Enlightenment Catholicism was a broad movement within German-speaking Catholicism and consequently boasted many religious leaders, thinkers, and activists. However, one person stands out above all others in this movement: Ignaz Heinrich Freiherr von Wessenberg, doubtless the most defamed and execrated of the Enlightenment Catholics (he was, among other things, quite an able poet; he published scores of his poems during his lifetime). He was born November 4, 1774, in Dresden, received a canonicat in

Constance in 1797, was appointed Vicar General of Constance by Archbishop Karl Theodor Anton Maria von Dalberg—who left to rule over a second archdiocese, Regensburg—in 1802, was ordained to the priesthood in 1812, after Archbishop Dalberg's death in 1817 was elected Chapter Vicar of Constance, and, despite Rome's opposition, remained the diocesan administrator until 1827. From 1819 to 1833 he was a member of the *Ständekammer* of the Duchy of Baden. He died on August 9, 1860. It must be noted that the diocese of Constance, of which Wessenberg was the de facto head, was far and away the largest diocese in the world! Hence, what he did there had a massive impact (more about this follows).

NOTES

1. Franz Schnabel, *Deutsche Geschichte im neunzehnten Jahrhundert*, vol. IV (Freiburg: Herder & Co., 1951, 2nd ed.), pp. 10 ff.

2. E.g., Adolf Rösch, *Das religiöse Leben in Hohenzollern unter den Einflüsse des Wessenbergianismus 1800–1850. Ein Beitrag zur Geschichte der religiösen Aufklärung in Süddeutschland.Görres-Gesellschaft zur Pflege der Wissenschaft im katholischen Deutschland. Zweite Vereinsschrift für 1908* (Cologne, 1908); and J. B. Sägmüller, *Wissenschaft und Glaube der kirchlichen Aufklärung (c. 1750–1850)* (Essen, 1910).

3. Georg May, *Interkonfessionalismus in der ersten Hälfte des 19. Jahrhunderts* (Paderborn: F. Shöningh, 1969), p. 9.

4. Waldemar Trapp, *Vorgeschichte und Ursprung der liturgischen Bewegung vorwiegend in Hinsicht auf das deutsche Sprachgebiet* (Würzburg: Buchdruckerei Richard Mayr, 1939), pp. 84ff.

5. *Der Katholik* (Mainz), vol. LXXIII, p. 155.

6. August Hagen, *Der Reformkatholizismus in der Diözese Rottenburg* (Stuttgart: Schwabenverlag, 1962).

7. Ernest Koenker, *The Liturgical Renaissance in the Roman Catholic Church* (Chicago: University of Chicago Press, 1954), pp. 21 ff.; Trapp, *Vorgeschichte*, pp. 357 ff.

· 2 ·

Enlightenment Reforms

ENLIGHTENMENT REFORM OF THE LITURGY

$\mathscr{B}$ecause it is in the liturgy that the average Catholic, especially when relatively uneducated, encounters his or her religion, liturgical reform was the spearhead of Enlightenment Catholicism. Consequently this liturgical reform was subsequently defamed. For example, on the first page of his history of the Liturgical Movement Dom Olivier Rousseau, OSB, stated:

> Let us understand that we are dealing with the true liturgical movement. . . . It has nothing in common, as we shall see, with a certain tendency of Jansenism and the Enlightenment, which at first sight it seems to resemble. The liturgical movement is, in fact, essentially opposed to such tendencies; for this reason, it has received the blessing of the Church. The "liturgical reforms" of Jansenism and the Enlightenment were a part of the general breakdown of Christian thought and merely another expression of eighteenth-century laicism.[1]

Such an attitude toward the attempts at liturgical reform undertaken in the eighteenth century and the early nineteenth century was typical not only for most twentieth-century Catholic scholars but also for all those who opposed liturgical reform in the period of the

Enlightenment and subsequently. Perhaps the first outstanding exception to this view is to be found in the excellent work by Waldemar Trapp.[2] Trapp has done an extraordinarily thorough research job into the liturgical reform efforts of the Enlightenment in Germany, and has been of invaluable assistance in the writing of this study. Moreover, he gives a sympathetic, balanced presentation of the positions of the Enlightenment Catholics, although some post–Vatican II Catholic scholars might think he darkens the shadows of the Enlightenment somewhat unduly because of pre-conciliar ecclesiastical pressures. It is of interest to note that Dom Rousseau's book mentioned above, which is condemnatory of the Enlightenment, does not make use of this work of Trapp's, although it was published some five years before Rousseau's.

During the latter half of the seventeenth century Catholics who promoted some kind of religious reform ran the serious risk of being categorized as Jansenist, which categorization, once Jansensim was condemned by Rome, could be used as an effective weapon against them and their reforms.

Jansenism stemmed from the Fleming Cornelius Jansen, the bishop of Ypres, whose single major work, *Augustinus,* appeared in 1640, two years after his death; it was mainly a study of the question of grace in the teaching of St. Augustine. It tended toward a rigoristic position and soon became the source of a vigorous theological controversy, which also quickly took on political dimensions. Louis XIV of France wanted a unified nation behind him for his various military adventures and hence attempted in various ways at different times to suppress the Jansenists. Doubtless part of the reason he opposed them was that they had become the champions of various religious reforms, and the virus of reform could spread too easily from the religious sphere to the political. The harassing of Jansenists, which included severe psychical and physical punishment of the nuns of the convent of Port-Royal in France, reached a high point with the papal bull *Unigenitus,* issued at the urging of Louis XIV in 1713 against the writings of the Jansenist Pasquier Quesnel. In *Uni-*

genitus 101 statements culled from the writings of Quesnel so as to form a sort of summary of Jansenist teaching were condemned. The condemned statements included: "To snatch from the simple people this consolation of joining their voice to the voice of the whole Church is a custom contrary to the apostolic practice and to the intention of God (Denz. 1436)"; and "The reading of Sacred Scripture is for all (Denz. 1430)." (Compare Vatican II Council's Dogmatic Constitution on Divine Revelation, par. 22: "Easy access to sacred scripture should be provided for all the Christian faithful.") Despite the enforced acceptance of the bull *Unigenitus*, the Jansenist influence was nevertheless felt in many places for many decades afterward. In sum, it should be noted that Jansenism was a very complex phenomenon; "Popular speech confuses it with rigorism, with which it is connected only in an accidental way."[3]

During the latter half of the eighteenth century and the first half of the nineteenth century a different constellation of motives and principles for liturgical reform became prominent—the Enlightenment. Because the Enlightenment was a vastly broader movement than Jansenism, whose very name indicates its personal origin, it could not so clearly be condemned by Rome. Nevertheless in the period of the Restoration, after the demise of the French Revolution in 1815, the term *Enlightenment* more and more became a weapon to be used against reforms and those who promoted them—much as the initially proud political term "liberal" was at the end of the twentieth century turned into a negative weapon by extreme conservative political elements in the United States.

The Enlightenment liturgical reform was exceedingly deep and broad. It covered such areas as preaching, the vernacular in the liturgy, the multiplicity of Masses, Eucharistic reforms, church music, church architecture, missal and Mass reforms, sacramental reforms, reform of the Ritual, extensive Breviary reforms, the battle against superstitions, pilgrimages and processions, fasting, the cult of saints, and Marian piety.[4] It definitely was not, however, a Protestantization of Catholic worship, with a tendency toward a sole focus on the "word." For example, Wolfgang Müller wrote of Wessenberg:

> It is absolutely not so that for Wessenberg divine worship is essentially completed in the sermon. His concept of the Holy Mass and its value was thoroughly conservative. It is noteworthy that he placed great value in having Holy Communion distributed during Mass; he recommended that even when a general reception of communion could not be expected at least several be encouraged to come forward to receive.[5]

The success the Enlightenment liturgical reform had was ably summed up in the words Wessenberg himself wrote to his clergy at the end of his administration of the diocese of Constance:

> Beloved brothers, colleagues, and friends in the Lord! When I review with calm earnestness the twenty-five years during which it was given to me to provide leadership for your struggles and efforts, it gives me a great deal of inner joy to be able to publicly bear an honorable witness to you that the condition of pastoral care has within that period of time improved itself immensely in many regards. The public veneration of God has received a more worthy form, a greater seriousness and order . . . [particularly through] the spread of a general song and devotion book . . . the preaching of the Divine Word has been brought into closer relationship again to the holy sacrifice of the Mass, as was the original intention and order of the Church. [The parish worship service as the common bond has been promoted and thus] has the worthy celebration of the Sundays and Holy Days essentially improved. . . . By means of Vesper devotions in the vernacular, congregational church prayers, litanies, and hymns, by the reading aloud of appropriate portions of the Scripture during afternoon devotions and prayer hours and processions, the soul-killing mechanical spirit has been confronted and the spirit and heart has been raised up in inner, joyful, and edifying adoration.

He then went on to speak of the improvements in the celebration of the sacraments:

> The salutary reception of the Sacraments of Penance and the Eucharist has been effectively fostered by appropriate liturgical celebrations. . . . This is particularly so in the case of the celebration of the Eucharist for children. . . . Likewise in the administration of the other holy Sacraments the understanding and power of edification of the ecclesiastical rites and ceremonies has received a certain happy increase . . . because they were administered with appropriate German instructions, prayers, and hymns. . . . Live up to your high calling . . . do everything for the sake of the Gospel, hold fast and unshakably onto that costly treasure, the Faith delivered to the Church, which has been entrusted to you! Listen to and love accordingly the Church as loyal, teachable children who with the greatest certitude walk with their hands in that of their loving mother![6]

ENLIGHTENMENT STRESS ON THE BIBLE

The Enlightenment has the reputation of making a rather simplistic concept of man's reason into the standard against which all things are to be measured. However, for Enlightenment Catholics the stress on reason did not mean the elimination of the belief in God's revelation as manifested through the Scriptures. In fact, Enlightenment Catholics stressed very strongly the importance of the Bible. However they stressed the need to get at the literal sense of the Bible, rather than the mystical or allegorical senses which were so very often popular in previous times. Consequently they also felt that it was very necessary to see to it that priests received a thorough grounding in Scriptural studies during their seminary training. How else could they fulfill one of their main functions, namely, that of preaching on the Scriptures at the Eucharistic celebration? But

Enlightenment Catholics did not stop at placing the Bible once more prominently in the hands of the priests. They also promoted the reading of the Bible very widely among the laity.[7] Here too the Enlightenment Catholics sounded very much like Vatican II Catholics.

CATECHETICAL AND EDUCATIONAL REFORMS

The first part of the nineteenth century stood at the brink of the Age of the Masses. The great mass education systems had not yet been established, but they were in the offing, with the work of such pioneers as Johann Heinrich Pestalozzi (1746–1827, born in Zurich, Switzerland, part of Wessenberg's diocese) at their bases. Logically following their notion that the liturgy was to instruct and motivate and that for the same purposes the Bible was to be widely distributed and employed, Enlightenment Catholics promoted mass education with all possible vigor, through both the churches and secular politics. Naturally also Enlightenment Catholics brought their concern for an improvement and spread of education in general to the very crucial matter of religious education, or catechetics.

Wessenberg, for example, insisted that his priests not only preach at the Eucharist but also give religious instructions outside Mass on a regular and frequent basis. Wessenberg also personally saw to it that his seminarians had regular instructions and experience not only in preaching during their seminary days but also in religious teaching.

He was a close friend of Pestalozzi himself and did everything he could to promote his new ideas and techniques. Pestalozzi wrote:

> I wish to wrest education from the outworn order of doddering old teaching hacks as well as from the newfangled order of cheap, artificial teaching tricks, and entrust it to the eternal powers of nature herself, to the light which God has kindled and kept

alive in the hearts of fathers and mothers, to the interests of parents who desire their children grow up in favour with God and with men.[8]

Pestalozzi put his ideas into practice, establishing a "psychological method of instruction" that matched the "laws of human nature." As a consequence he stressed spontaneity and self-activity. Children were not to be given canned answers but they should arrive at answers themselves; they should use their own powers of seeing and judging, and reasoning should be fostered by educating the whole child: "The aim is to educate the whole child—intellectual education is only part of a wider plan. He looked to balance, or keep in equilibrium, three elements—hands, heart, and head."[9]

Wessenberg, and other Enlightenment theologians, inspired by these ideas and practices, also wrote new catechisms. To promote this enterprise in his own diocese Wessenberg offered prizes for the best catechisms written; he found many takers. Arrangements were made to give special instructions in the new catechetical techniques to priests already in the field. The status of the teacher was raised, and priests were cautioned to relinquish their clerical privilege and to become "a friend of the teacher."

Thus, like post–Vatican II Catholics, who experienced a catechetical renewal, Enlightenment Catholics also placed great stress on the vital importance of religious instruction and updating the training of the priests and teachers in theology in general, but most particularly in the areas of biblical studies and in the study of church history and the history of doctrines and the employment of the latest techniques of education.[10]

THEOLOGICAL REFORM

Enlightenment Catholics, as their name indicates, felt that new light needed to be shed on the area of theology, making use of the best of contemporary philosophical thought. Consequently they were very critical of Scholasticism or what at least passed for Scholasticism at that time. Although for the most part, the majority of Enlightenment churchmen engaged in what they considered to be practical reforms rather than doctrinal reforms, a number of teachings were very widely criticized by them. Indulgences, for example, were often thought to be conducive to superstition and hence to be eliminated. The devil came in for a particularly hard time and was most often transformed into a sort of mythical personification of evil in the abstract. Hence, for example, the exorcism in the administration of Baptism as found in Wessenberg's new *Ritual* was directed against evil rather than the devil as a person.[11] Some Enlightenment churchmen, such as Father Benedict Werkmeister, stated that the doctrine of transubstantiation was not one that Catholics were bound to hold (this stance anticipated the work of the highly respected contemporary Catholic theologians Schoonenberg and Schillebeeckx, and others, who developed similar positions, by some 150 years).

Besides the churchmen of the Enlightenment, who were mostly interested in practical church reforms, there were several academic theologians who strove for the reform of theology in the Enlightenment spirit. One of the most important was Johann Adam Möhler, who was born on May 6, 1796, in Jägersheim bei Mergentheim in Württemberg, part of what was to become Wessenberg's diocese. He became a priest in 1819, in 1826 became an Extraordinary Professor, in 1828 became an Ordinary Professor of Church History in the newly reestablished Catholic Theological Faculty at the University of Tübingen, became the same at the University of Munich in 1835, and died on April 12, 1838, in Munich. In his early years as a young professor Möhler was strongly *Aufgeklärt* (Enlightened), as was reflected in his 1826 book *Die Einheit in der Kirche* (The Unity in the Church) and his reviews and articles in the *Tübinger Quartalschrift* (before 1828, when the anti-celibacy movement appeared to be the rock on which his reform spirit, if it did not break, at least bent very badly).

Another *aufgeklärter* theologian was Möhler's colleague at Tübingen, Johannes Baptist Hirscher, whose focus was moral and pastoral theology. Hirscher was born on January 20, 1788, in Altergarten by Ravensburg, was ordained to the priesthood in 1810, and became Professor of Moral and Pastoral Theology in Tübingen in 1817, then Professor of Moral Theology in Freiburg im Breisgau from 1837 to 1863, a member of the Cathedral Chapter in 1839, and the Cathedral Dean in Freiburg in 1850. He died September 4, 1865. His efforts at promoting the use of the vernacular in the liturgy earned a place for some of his books on Rome's *Index of Forbidden Books.*

In addition, there were three more philosophical theologians who undertook a theoretical approach to theology in the spirit of the Enlightenment, of reason and reform. One was Bernard Bolzano (1781–1848), who taught *Religionswissenschaft* at the University of Prague the first two decades of the nineteenth century until he was removed in 1821. Bolzano, who was also an outstanding theoretical mathematician, developed pioneer philosophical directions in linguistic analysis, philosophy of religion, and social ethics. He narrowly escaped being placed on the Index by name and being suspended (years-long efforts by supporters and timely deaths of enemies saved him), and continued throughout his life to be a power for reform in Austrian Catholicism through his disciples, his scholarly work, and his correspondence.[12]

A second theoretical theologian imbued with the Enlightenment spirit was Georg Hermes (1775–1831). He was appointed Professor of Theology at the University of Münster in 1807, and at the new University of Bonn in 1820. All his scholarly efforts were bent toward putting a thoroughly rational foundation under Catholic theology. In this he was supported by Baron Ferdinand August von Spiegel, the Archbishop of Cologne; his teaching and writings earned him very many followers who were quickly appointed to professorships:

Like the theological faculty at Bonn, to which only pupils of Hermes had been appointed since 1826 (Archterfeldt, Braun,

Vogelsang, Willer), the seminary at Cologne and a large part of the clergy were soon imbued with his ideas. Even the other faculties of Bonn included followers of his, particularly, Professor Clement August von Droste-Hülshoff in law and Elvenich in philosophy. In a very short time the theological faculties of Breslau, Münster, and Braunsberg, the seminary at Trier, many cathedral chapters, and instructorships in religion at the gymnasia were filled with Hermensians. . . . Achterfeldt and Siemers wrote for use in the higher schools' textbooks of religious instructions incorporating his views. . . . The Archbishop of Cologne, Baron von Spiegel, continued to champion Hermesianism even after the death of its author, and he silenced by repeated favorable reports the doubts that had been awakened in Rome as to the correctness of the new doctrine.[13]

The archbishop died in 1835 (upon which "Pope Gregory XVI piously remarked, 'Hence it is fortunate that this archbishop is dead, who at any rate was basically a bad bishop.'"[14]) and a few weeks later a thoroughgoing condemnation of Hermes' works was issued by Rome. Spiegel's successor, the very conservative and authoritarian Clement August von Droste Vischering (an early personal foe of Hermes), rammed through an elimination of all the disciples and influences of Hermes within his jurisdiction, and even beyond.

The third theoretical theologian who worked to reform theology in the spirit of the Enlightenment and reason (though with strong influences of idealistic philosophy) was Anton Günther (1783–1863), who lived most of his life in Vienna. He too gained a large following among Catholic academic philosophers and theologians all across Austria and Germany. But Günther's work also fell before the condemnation of the Congregation of the Index in 1857 for a variety of reasons, but particularly, as Pope Pius IX wrote, because of its "fundamental rationalism, which is the controlling factor of his philosophy even in the handling of Christian dogmas."[15] Many of Günther's followers joined the Old Catholic Church when it was formed in opposition to the dogma of papal infallibility declared in 1870.

It seems that every effort to re-think the Christian faith in contemporary thought patterns is resisted by authority, by Rome (as all paradigm shifts are in all areas of thought). So it happened to these theologians who tried to re-think the faith in Enlightenment thought categories. It happened again to the Enlightenment Catholicism Redivivus at the beginning of the twentieth century in the anti-Modernist heresy hunt unleashed after 1907 by Pope Pius X. It happened also to the beginning of Enlightenment Catholicism Re-Redivivus, that is, when there was an extraordinary flowering of creative Catholic theology in the decade and a half leading up to Vatican II and in the several decades afterward—again, despite the constant oppression of Rome. Concerning the latter, one thinks of the outstanding theologians of the Vatican II era such as Jean Danielou, Henri De Lubac, Yves Congar, John Courtney Murray, Karl Rahner, Hans Küng, Edward Schillebeeckx, Bernard Häring . . . all of whom had been investigated, or even silenced, by the Vatican. More of this follows.

ECUMENISM

When the history of the ecumenical movement is recounted, it is most often stated that it began with the Protestant world missionary conference at Edinburgh in 1910. Earlier roots in the nineteenth century are of course also traced and sometimes a nod is given in the direction of the exchange of letters between the Protestant thinker Leibniz and Catholic Bishop Bossuet in the latter part of the seventeenth century. However, with the exception of a Catholic or two here or there, such as Bishop Bossuet, the participation of the Roman Catholic Church in ecumenism is usually said to have begun in

Germany only shortly after the First World War with the "Una Sancta Movement."[16]

However here too the Enlightenment Catholics of Germany are again overlooked. For example, 130 years before John XXIII announced the calling of Vatican II to renew the Church so as to be ready for Christian reunion, Fridolin Huber (1763–1841) of Wessenberg's diocese and for a while (1827–28) even the rector of the seminary at Rottenburg wrote that he and his many colleagues were working vigorously for reform within the Roman Catholic Church not only for its own sake but also in the hope that through the elimination of the glaring defects within the Catholic Church the reasons for the division between Catholics and Protestants would thereby disappear. Indeed even some forty years before that the Enlightenment Catholic prince par excellence, Emperor Joseph II of Austria, also felt that as the Catholic Church was purified Protestants would reunite with it in corporate fashion.

Vatican II's second great ecumenical document, the "Declaration on Religious Liberty," was also anticipated by the Enlightenment Catholics in their constant insistence on religious freedom and freedom of conscience. This religious freedom was also extended by them specifically to Jews, a freedom not fully enjoyed by Jews even after 1965 in Roman Catholic Spain, even though it was mandated in Vatican II's decree on non-Christian religions.

In ecumenism the Enlightenment Catholics most naturally were primarily concerned with Protestants. At a time when Roman Catholic churchmen were still writing of Martin Luther as something akin to the devil incarnate we find that a number of Enlightenment churchmen and theologians exhibited a great deal of sympathy for Luther in his concern for, and attempt to reform, the Catholic Church. One of the Catholic Enlightenment reformers even promoted a very ambitious plan for the reunion of the Catholic and Protestant Churches. He suggested that Catholic and Protestant congregations alternately use the same place of worship and that they also have an exchange of preachers so that they might hear about each other's beliefs and practices in an authentic, irenic manner. Gradually they would develop a kind of joint liturgical community, and eventually this road would lead to unity.

Benedikt Maria Werkmeister, the author of this plan, was able to put some of these ideas into action, although in a very limited fashion, in Stuttgart where he was one of the court chaplains. Werkmeister was born October 22, 1745, in Füssen in Bavaria, entered the Benedictine monastery of Neresheim in Allgäu in 1764, was ordained to the priesthood in 1769, became novice master and professor of philosophy both at his monastery and the Lyzeum in Freising in 1770, became Court Preacher in Stuttgart in 1784, and in 1790 left the order, with papal permission. In 1796 he became pastor in Steinbach in Württemberg, and Chief Church Counsel in Stuttgart in 1817. He died on July 16, 1823.

It was the same Werkmeister who was able to arrange to bring Protestant and Catholic religion teachers and also Protestant and Catholic clergy together to study the education methods of Pestalozzi. In commenting on what he had already accomplished in this joint Catholic and Protestant study Werkmeister rejoiced that the barriers between the confessions were coming down to some extent and hoped that they would continue to do so.

Such joint Protestant and Catholic endeavors in the religious field deepened as the century developed. In the 1830s a theological journal was founded by clergymen aimed at both Protestant and Catholic clerics with the editorial team being made up of both Protestant and Catholic clergymen. The new hymnbooks produced by Enlightenment Catholics also reflected the more open attitude toward Protestantism in that they now freely borrowed from Protestant hymnbooks as well as older Catholic ones.[17]

MIXED MARRIAGE

The question of mixed marriage was as vexing a problem two hundred years ago as it is today. Enlightenment Catholics felt that to take the rigid Catholic stand on mixed marriage, that is, that all the children must be raised in the Catholic Church, was, among other things, destructive of the possibility of church reunion. They also felt that such an insistence on the Catholic side was a basic violation of justice and the conscience of the Protestant partner. They even went to the length of feeling that such mixed marriages entered into in the proper spirit would provide the seeds of religious freedom and respect. Wessenberg even saw to it that in his diocese both the Protestant and Catholic clergymen would be involved in the mixed marriage ceremony; namely, the marriage ceremony was always first performed before the minister of the bridegroom and then afterward before the minister of the bride. But in many other instances the marriage ceremony was conducted jointly by the two clergymen.[18]

There are of course now many modifications of the earlier rigid Catholic position, allowing non-Catholic clergy a variety of roles in the marriage ceremony, and the old written promise concerning the raising of the children Catholic has been lifted. Once again, Enlightenment Catholicism was there before.

RESTRUCTURING PAPAL GOVERNMENT

Enlightenment Catholics realized that basic changes in the structure of the Catholic Church were necessary to put through far-reaching reforms. This stress on structural changes was a particularly central theme in the work and writings of the long-lived Wessenberg, who was active from the beginning of the nineteenth century until after the mid-century mark. These structural reform efforts by him and other Enlightenment Catholics earned them the ire of the Vatican. To this day Wessenberg's reputation has been so maligned that he is almost never heard of by Catholics, and when he is, it is usually in denigrating fashion. The same is true of Werkmeister and other of the Enlightenment theologians and churchmen. It is not merely that their values were held in disdain by contemporary conservatives but that quite incredible lies were told about them.[19]

In response, of course the Enlightenment Catholics filled their writing with the severest criticisms of Rome, particularly of the Curia and curialist theology and tactics of domination. The earlier mentioned papal encyclical *Mirari vos* issued in 1832 delivered the coup de grace to budding liberal Catholicism in France, but it met with a bitter reaction and criticism from the German Enlightenment Catholics.[20] Enlightenment Catholics felt very strongly that the claims and pretensions of Rome should be vastly scaled down, that the papal office was to be one of unity rather than authoritarian domination. The role of the local bishop vis-à-vis Rome was to be one of much greater independence, and much greater stress was placed on the bishops of individual nations acting together in joint fashion,[21] not unlike the way post–Vatican II national episcopal conferences do.

THE "SYNODAL MOVEMENT"

However, Enlightenment Catholics were not content with scaling down the power claims of Rome in favor of the bishop; they also wished to eliminate the authoritarian claims of power on the part of the bishop as well. Enlightenment Catholics wanted all of the elements within the Church to participate in the decision making of the Church. Hence, they argued that the bishop should act conjointly with his presbyterium of clergy, that associations or conferences of clergy should be set up to meet regularly, and that diocesan synods made up of lay and clerical representatives of the whole diocese ought to be called to help decide the most pressing questions of the day.[22] In sum, Enlightenment Catholics promoted a great deal more freedom and responsibility for *all* elements within the Church. A whole series of petitions for synodal governments was organized in south-west Germany in the 1830s and '40s, known throughout Germany as the "synodal movement." Today in Catholic Church history writings, however, one can hardly find a mention of it, even though it produced a number of new titles for the *Index of Forbidden Books*.[23]

It is interesting to note that as a strong authoritarian counter-movement developed in the 1830s and '40s on the wave of a general cultural backlash the Enlightenment Catholics were strongly criticized by their opponents as being "unchurchly." In fact, the anti-Enlightenment movement was known then and subsequently by conservative Catholic writers as the "churchly" movement, *die kirchliche Bewegung*. When one looks carefully at what these writers both then and since meant by *kirchlich*, it is clear that the touchstone was whether or not a person spoke and acted totally in favor of authoritarian government in the hands of the bishop and the Vatican. In the pontificate of Pope John Paul II history is repeated itself.

CLERICAL CELIBACY

In the 1820s and particularly in the 1830s there was an extraordinarily strong movement to lift the law of mandatory clerical celibacy, with a flood of literature on the subject and a great deal of support on the part of educated laity, and most importantly, on the part of huge numbers of priests and theologians. In the diocese of Freiburg im Breisgau in southwestern Germany alone a number of petitions over a several-year period were sent in, sometimes to the archbishop and sometimes even to the state legislature, which at that time had a great deal to do with church affairs. One such petition in the early 1840s was signed by over six hundred of the diocesan clergy in the diocese of Freiburg, more than two-thirds of the secular clergy in that diocese. The entire Catholic theology faculty of the University of Freiburg supported the lifting of mandatory clerical celibacy, and did so both in their individual writings and publications and also in the signing of petitions.[24]

As indicated above, I am convinced that it was this optional celibacy movement that broke the commitment of Johann Adam Möhler to Enlightenment Catholicism. All of his frequent articles and reviews in the *Tübinger Quartalschrift* were vigorously critical of Rome. However, he never wrote in favor of eliminating clerical celibacy when the movement surfaced in 1828. In fact, he suddenly ceased writing altogether for over two years. Then when he did write again it was neither in favor of optional celibacy nor any longer critical of Rome; further, he soon left Tübingen and went to Munich where he produced his theologically much more conservative book *Symbolik.* It appears that Möhler came up against a personal decision: to remain in the priesthood, and therefore celibate, or to throw both over. Apparently he was not comfortable remaining a celibate priest while criticizing the celibate priesthood, and hence moved moderately to the right psychologically and theologically.

SECULAR MORAL ISSUES

Enlightenment Catholics were concerned not only with internal reform of the Catholic Church but also with the current moral issues, which they felt included the need for a great deal more freedom and responsibility in the political spheres—that is, such things as freedom of the press, freedom of speech, freedom of assembly, representative government, and promotion of education. Quite naturally the area of moral concern for the Enlightenment Catholics also included those centering on sex, as for example priestly celibacy. The problem of divorce and remarriage was very much discussed by Enlightenment Catholics, and they clearly came down on the side of the need for allowing divorce and remarriage where marriage has been a failure.[25]

The central questions of freedom were very much on the minds and hearts of many in Europe, and America, since the eighteenth century and the legacy of the French Revolution—which the Vatican increasingly resisted as the nineteenth century wore on. More of that follows, but here let me recall that freedom was also a central concern of Vatican II. In his famous triumphal first lecture tour of the United States in 1963, Hans Küng delivered everywhere a lecture to sold-out halls on "Freedom and Unfreedom." Though freedom appeared to gain the upper hand at Vatican II, the hand of repression has been squeezing ever more tightly in the decades thereafter. As in the secular sphere, the struggle for freedom is never ending.

NOTES

1. Olivier Rousseau, *The Progress of the Liturgy* (Westminster, Md.: Newman Press, 1951), p. vii. The original French version was published in 1944.

2. Waldemar Trapp, *Vorgeschichte und Ursprung der liturgischen Bewegung vorwiegend in Hinsicht auf das deutsche Sprachgebiet* (Würzburg: Buchdruckerei Richard Mayr, 1939).

3. *New Catholic Encyclopedia*, article on Jansenism.

4. For details see Leonard Swidler, *Aufklärung Catholicism 1780-1850. Liturgical and Other Reforms in the Catholic Aufklärung. American Academy of Religion Studies in Religion* 17 (Missoula, Mont.: Scholars Press, 1978). The table of contents lists the following topics of *Aufklärung* liturgical reform: 1. Jansenist Inspired Reforms 2. The *Aufklärung* 3. Mechanical Ritualism 4. Morality and Liturgy 5. Instruction and Motivation 6. Preaching 7. The Vernacular in the Liturgy 8. Theologians in Favor of the Vernacular 9. Churchmen in Favor of the Vernacular 10. Reaction against the Vernacular 11. *Aufklärung* Stress on Community 12. The Multiplicity of Masses 13. Eucharistic Reforms 14. Church Music 15. Church Architecture 16. Missal and Mass Reforms 17. Sacramental Reforms (a. Baptism, b. Penance, c. Confirmation) 18. Reform of the Ritual 19. Extensive Breviary Reforms 20. Battle against Superstitions 21. Pilgrimages and Processions 22. Fasting 23. Cult of Saints 24. Marian Piety 25. Conclusion.

5. "Wessenberg in heutiger Sicht," *Zeitschrift für Schweizerische Kirchengeschichte*, vol. LVIII (1964), p. 298.

6. Ignaz Heinrich von Wessenberg, "Allgemeiner Rezess über die Akten der Pastoral-konferenzen," *Archiv für Pastoralkonferenzen in den Landkapiteln des Bistums Konstanz* vol. I (Freiburg, 1827), pp. 4–28.

7. Hermann Lauer, *Geschichte der katholischen Kirche im Grossherzogtum Baden* (Freiburg: Herder, 1908), p. 63.

8. K. Silber, *Pestalozzi: The Man and His Work*, 2nd ed. (London: Routledge and Paul Kegan, 1965), p. 134.

9. www.infed.org/thinkers/et-pest.htm(Mark K. Smith, 2004).

10. Joseph Beck, *Freiherr I. Heinrich v. Wessenberg Sein Leben und Wirken* (Freiburg, 1862), pp. 103 ff.

11. Ibid., pp. 134 ff.

12. Cf. Eduard Winter, *Bernard Bolzano und sein Kreis* (Leipzig: J. Hegner, 1933).

13. Joseph Schulte, "Hermes," *The Catholic Encyclopedia* (New York, 1910), vol. VII, p. 277.

14. Eduard Winter, *Josefinismus* (Berlin: Rütten & Loening, 1962), p. 273.

15. Friedrich Lauchert, "Günther," *The Catholic Encyclopedia* (New York, 1910), vol. VII, p. 87.

16. For a history of the Una Sancta Movement and the ecumenical movement in general up to Vatican II, see Leonard Swidler, *The Ecumenical Vanguard* (Pittsburgh: Duquesne University Press, 1965).

17. For a very antagonistic overview, see Georg May, *Interkonfessionalismus in der ersten Hälfte des 19. Jahrhunderts* (Paderborn: F. Schöningh, 1969).

18. Ibid., pp. 42 ff.

19. August Hagen, *Die kirchliche Aufklärung in der Diözese Rottenburg* (Stuttgart, 1953), pp. 9 ff.

20. Ferdinand Strobel, *Der Katholizismus und die liberalen Strömungen in Baden vor 1848* (Munich, 1938), pp. 106f.

21. Ibid., pp. 102 ff.

22. Ibid., pp. 117–19, 145–52.

23. E.g., Johann Baptist von Hirscher, *Die kirchlichen Zustände der Gegenwart* (Tübingen, 1849).

24. Strobel, *Katholizimus*, pp. 73–81; Lauer, *Gesschichte*, pp. 140–43.

25. Lauer, *Geschichte*, p. 88.

· 3 ·

Extent and Demise
of Enlightenment Catholicism

THE EXTENT AND
VARIETY OF ENLIGHTENMENT CATHOLICISM

The greatest stronghold of Enlightenment Catholicism was the diocese of Constance, since the seventh century the largest diocese in area and population in Germany and in the world. It included southwestern present-day Germany and the great majority of German-speaking Switzerland, extending from the Rhine on the west, and the St. Gotthard pass on the south, to the Iller River on the east up through Ulm, Gmünd, and across the Neckar River north of Marbach. In 1435 the diocese had 17,060 priests, 1,760 parishes, and 350 monasteries and convents. There were many losses in the Reformation, but in 1750 there were still 3,774 secular priests, 2,764 monks, 3,147 nuns, and a Catholic population of 891,948.[1] In 1805, when Wessenberg took charge, there were "about one and a half million Catholics, about a third of whom were in Baden. The total clergy numbered 6,608 persons, including 2,365 secular priests, for the most part employed in the care of souls or teaching, 1,220 non-mendicant monks, 906 from different mendicant orders, and 2,117 nuns. There were therefore 233 persons per cleric!"[2]

In reading over the literature of the first part of the nineteenth century one finds that the great majority of the clergy of southwestern Germany, the entire Catholic theology faculty of the University of Freiburg, almost half of the Catholic theologians of the University of Tübingen in Württemberg, the majority of the Catholic theology faculty of the University of Bonn, and many other Catholic theologians elsewhere in Germany and Austria were judged Enlightenment Catholics at the beginning of the 1830s. The same was true also of the rector of the seminary in southwestern Germany, as well as the director of the teacher-training institution in southwestern Germany, and also the vast majority of the grammar and high school teachers and very many of the journalists and publishers. Hence in the beginning of the 1830s the intellectual, educational, and clerical communities were overwhelmingly Enlightenment Catholics, at least in southwestern Germany and also in many other areas of German-speaking lands. Moreover, there was at least a certain amount of mutual support and collaboration in the reform efforts of Enlightenment Catholics in various parts of the Germanies.[3]

One twentieth-century German scholar antagonistic to the Enlightenment, Ferdinand Strobel, granted that the extent of the spread of the spirit of the Enlightenment among the common folk is difficult to gauge, and then referred to an earlier scholar as arguing that "only from around 1830 on were the majority of the people completely taken up by the Enlightenment. He therefore places the highpoint of the Enlightenment between 1830 and 1850."[4] Strobel, in speaking of Baden, nevertheless argued that many of the common folk were opposed to the Enlightenment in church matters even though they "were corrupted by political liberalism" in political matters. No persuasive evidence is provided, however, especially in view of his admission of all the strengths of the Enlightenment listed above, including that "until 1840 the majority of the clergy still declared for the Enlightenment and even went so far as to state that 'the majority of *Volksschule* teachers appeared to be the source of radicalism.'"[5] If all that is true, it is difficult to see how the Enlightenment could not have had a significant influence on the general population—which was taught and led for so many years by these clergy, teachers, etc.

Hermann Lauer makes just this differentiated point:

> Wessenberg's reforms were received very differently by the
> Catholic *Volk*. The *aufgeklärte* circles of the cities received
> Wessenberg enthusiastically and praised his merits to the stars.
> The reforms also found a favorable reception with a part of the
> country people, that is, where an otherwise diligent pastor con-
> cerned about school and undertakings helpful to the community
> knew how to present them in a favorable light. But another part
> of the people anguished under them. They could not understand
> why all of a sudden the old handed-down religious customs
> should be tossed into the waste basket. They persistently resis-
> ted the reforms and vigorously opposed the reform clergy. . . .
> Finally, however, the opposition of the people in most places
> was overcome.[6]

The moderate conservative church historian August Hagen wrote:

> How far the *Volk* were contaminated with the Enlightenment is
> difficult to say. The route would have been by way of the En-
> lightenment clergy and the Enlightenment publications. That
> communities in which such clergy worked for a long time fell
> under this spirit can be documented. The effect is to be traced
> to this very day. Certainly that did not include the majority of
> the communities of the diocese of Rottenburg. It is true that
> many catechisms of the Enlightenment were left untouched at
> that time, but the churchly catechisms held the upper hand—
> according to a survey from the year of 1841.[7]

As noted earlier, the reform movement among Enlightenment
Catholics in the first half of the nineteenth century in Germany was
not uniform. There were some extreme left elements among the reform movements, although usually not as extreme as they have often
been painted by conservative Catholic churchmen and historians.
But by far the vast majority of the Enlightenment Catholics were
what might be described accurately as moderate reformers: that is,

they wished to reform the Catholic Church; they very definitely rejected the idea of breaking with it. When, for example, in the middle 1840s a small group of left-wing Catholics broke away to form what was known as "German Catholicism," they were for the most part rejected by Enlightenment Catholics, with one of their great leaders, Wessenberg, in the forefront of this rejection.[8]

It should be clear, at least in outline fashion, that Vatican II and post–Vatican II Liberal Catholicism had an extraordinary predecessor in Enlightenment Catholicism, not only in the reform of the liturgy, but also in the stress on the Bible; the development of ecumenism; catechetical reform; critiques of dogmas with the use of contemporary thought; severe criticism of centralized authoritarianism, particularly curialism, and authoritarian episcopal power; the promotion of synodal and democratic government; the emphasizing of the importance of the laity; and the rethinking of many moral problems such as freedom and responsibility, celibacy, mixed marriages, and divorce. Moreover, in some areas, particularly in southwestern Germany, Enlightenment Catholicism had the support of the great majority of the theologians, the clergy, the teachers, and the educated laity. In short, it had the support basically of every level of society except that of the bishopric and Rome. So long as Wessenberg was the Administrator of the diocese of Constance, from 1802 to 1827, even one bishopric was on its side.

THE DEMISE OF ENLIGHTENMENT CATHOLICISM

However, Rome saw to it first of all that Wessenberg was never consecrated a bishop, and hence it was possible to have him removed from his position as Administrator in 1827. But even before that, Rome gradually restricted his area of influence by breaking up and diminishing in size the diocese of Constance in several operations. In 1814 the large Swiss district was removed from the diocese, and in 1817, after the death of the Bishop, Dalberg, the Bavaria and Württemberg districts were also removed; in 1821 the diocese was totally dissolved and attached to the newly erected archdiocese of Freiburg in Breisgau, though this latter move could not be implemented until 1827 when the state of Baden allowed Wessenberg to be removed as Administrator of the diocese of Constance. Clearly most of this dismemberment was designed to cut away all diocesan control by Wessenberg (at each step of the way Wessenberg's name was proposed as bishop, but each time it was rejected by the Vatican, at times with great protracted battles).

Hence in 1830, although Enlightenment Catholics did not have the support of any episcopal see in southwestern Germany, or anywhere else for that matter, they did seem to have the upper hand on other levels; yet by 1842 all eight of the Enlightenment Catholics who made up the Catholic theology faculty of the University of Freiburg in 1830 were eliminated by one sort of intrigue or another.[9] Conservatives were placed in the positions of rectors of seminaries and directors of the teacher-training institutions. As a result, by the latter part of the 1840s the conservative elements in Roman Catholicism were priding themselves on the great triumphs that they were enjoying. The new priests that were being turned out were *kirchlich*, that is, authoritarian, in their attitudes; the same was true of the new teachers being trained. The many Enlightenment journals and newspapers that flourished in the early 1830s had pretty well dried up and disappeared by 1850.[10] New Rituals being put into use were marked by the ever-greater use of Latin. The general result was that if one were to compare the Catholicism of 1855 with the Catholicism of twenty-five years earlier, the difference would have been like night and day. Enlightenment Catholicism seemed to have been almost entirely obliterated in a short time after it appeared to have an unbreakable hold on what one would think were nine-tenths of the key areas.

A comparison of this condition with the situation in Catholic America in 2007, after the more than quarter of a century pontificate of Pope John Paul II, evinces a striking resemblance in many regards. All but the most senior bishops now in place in America have been appointed by John Paul II, and by the judgment of a number of the older bishops, are not only almost always very conservative, but also very often quite incompetent as administrators. The massive ongoing scandal of the gross mismanagement of clergy sexual abuse by a significant number of bishops bears witness to this judgment.

In addition, a type of censorship has been imposed on candidates for the priesthood: they may not have written or spoken in a questioning manner about contemporary subjects like women priests, divorce and remarriage, priestly celibacy, homosexuality, and so on. When this restriction is imposed on candidates for the priesthood, then the collective mind of the priesthood atrophies even further. And it is from this limited pool that bishops are chosen.

Likewise, the pool of candidates for the priesthood in North America and Europe in the wake of Vatican II has drastically shrunk not only quantitatively but also qualitatively. There is vast evidence that very many of the priests ordained in the past two decades are very much of a "churchly" mentality, that is, rigid yes-men who are strongly authoritarian in mentality. Likewise, serious efforts by the Vatican have been made to try to rein in the teaching and teachers of theology on both the primary/secondary and higher education levels, as in the time of Enlightenment Catholicism.

However, things are also dramatically different at the beginning of the twenty-first century. I was probably the first Catholic layperson in modern times to receive a degree in Catholic theology (S.T.L. in 1959 from the Pontifical Catholic Theology Faculty of the University of Tübingen, Germany), but now there are thousands of such Catholic laypersons with advanced degrees in Catholic theology. As a group we are clearly vastly better educated in Catholic theology than the great majority of priests and bishops—indeed, better educated theologically than the majority of members of the Congregation for the Doctrine of the Faith.

NOTES

1. Michael Ott, "Constance," *The Catholic Encyclopedia* (New York, 1910), vol. IV, p. 287.

2. Beck, *Freiherr.*, pp. 94 ff.

3. Strobel, *Katholizismus*, pp. 92 ff.; cf. Trapp, *Vorgeschichte*, pp. 19–21.

4. Strobel, *Katholizismus*, p. 47; Strobel's reference is to Hermann Lauer, but no documentation is given at that point.

5. Ibid., pp. 47, 93.

6. Lauer, *Geschichte*, pp. 94–96.

7. August Hagen, *Geschichte der Diözese Rottenburg* (Stuttgart: Schwabenverlag, 1956), p. 61.

8. Heinrich Maas, *Geschichte der katholischen Kirche im Grossherzogthum Baden* (Freiburg: Herder, 1891), pp. 153 ff.

9. Strobel, *Katholizismus*, pp. 86 ff.

10. Ibid., pp. 18 ff.

· 4 ·

Reflection on the Anti-Enlightenment Attack

$\mathcal{A}$ reflective remark is in order at this point. Given the facts that the memory of Enlightenment Catholicism was at first most hostilely attacked and then almost wiped out by the near silence of subsequent Catholic Church historians, and given the restored image of Enlightenment Catholicism of the preceding pages that looks so extraordinarily like Vatican II Catholicism, certain questions naturally arise: Were there no plausible grounds on which the opponents of Enlightenment Catholicism based their opposition? Does it not border on the incredible that so many highly placed responsible Catholic ecclesiastical leaders, theologians, and historians could have taken actions so distorting and suppressive of facts?

Clearly the majority of the opponents of Enlightenment Catholicism very likely were not evil men, men of "bad will"—though one must not totally discount Lord Acton's dictum about power corrupting and absolute power corrupting absolutely. However, security is a basic human need. To attain and retain it, myriads of institutions are developed and preserved. When a wide range of the fundamental institutions of a society are suddenly threatened, the involuntary reaction of most people, including, or rather especially, most leaders, is fear and forceful reestablishment of the tottering institutions.

The end of the eighteenth century and first portion of the nineteenth century saw just such a profound shaking of many of the taken-for-granted institutions of Christendom. Already during the eighteenth-century Enlightenment in France (though *not* in Germany) the Catholic Church was being attacked from many sides under the banner of liberty. During the French Revolution, with its slogan of *liberté, fraternité, egalité,* the Church was severely ravaged —and not merely on the physical level. Priests and religious were persecuted, exiled, and murdered. Church property was desecrated— some being rededicated to the goddess of reason—and confiscated all over France. The situation was only somewhat ameloriated by Napoleon—the same Napoleon who kidnapped and browbeat Pope Pius VII.

But the Church's troubles were only just starting. The movement of democratic liberalism in its wider nineteenth-century sense cut away at the very foundation of the authoritarian, hierarchical structure of the Church and of society in general. This was followed by the more "perverse" movement of socialism, which would destroy the very basis of society—and hence the Church—that is, private property. And as if this were not enough, there then came the "satanic" development of Communism—the embodiment of materialism and atheism. Add to this the fact that the period between 1815 and 1870 was constantly filled with revolutions all over Europe and North and South America, the development of anarchism, scientism, evolutionism, and Protestant "liberal theology" with its debunking of the Bible as a Jesus myth foisted upon humanity by a dozen Jewish fishermen, and one will begin to see why so many nineteenth-ccentury Catholics were in a panic. Nothing seemed certain; nothing seemed stable anymore. Everything appeared to be washed away in the deluge of revolution and -isms that swept across nineteenth-century Europe. In terror people frantically searched for something stable. Many Catholics found it in an authoritarian Church with its structured-from-above hierarchy and the papacy at its apex. The cry among many seemed to be, "To Peter, to the Rock!"

An impenetrable bastion was built around the Rock fortress, and the condemned world was shut out. Until better times would come, only invectives and sallies were to come forth from the Rock.

It was within this context that the fearful opponents of Enlightenment Catholics viewed their reform efforts. Of course, as noted, there were extreme, reductionist notions advocated by some Enlightenment Catholics, as for example, Johann Anton Theiner (though in fact they were amazingly few, as indicated in the above pages). But the presence of such relatively extreme elements cannot possibly explain the extraordinarily strong reaction that developed against this basically reforming, not revolutionary, movement. Every movement of any magnitude, conservative or liberal, will have its relatively extreme elements. But the overwhelming crescendo of the Catholic anti-Enlightenment forces in the 1830s and following can be understood only within the broader cultural context of political, social, and intellectual reaction. That was the "Age of Metternich," the "Age of the Holy Alliance" of the Prussian, Russian, and Austrian Emperors reacting against the Jacobins, Decembrists, and Garibaldi's Red Shirts. In Catholicism it was also the Age of Gregory XVI and Pius IX, of *Mirari vos*, the Syllabus of Errors, and Papal Infallibility.

Even granting the fear, at times panic, of the men of the Establishment, there is still the question of whether they could have been responsible for such gross condemnations of Enlightenment Catholicism, of such totally black-and-white distinctions, of such complete assumptions of the insincerity and even evil of Enlightenment Catholics. No systematic attempt has been made in this study to provide representative quotations of the vilification of the Enlightenment Catholic reformers, nor will the space be taken to do so now. It will be sufficient, I believe, to allude to the leadership given the opponents of reforming efforts in Catholicism by the papacy. In 1832, early in his sixteen-year-long pontificate, Pope Gregory XVI made it clear that the "reform" of the Catholic Church was not even something to be desired, let alone tolerated or encouraged:

> It is obviously absurd and injurious to her [the Catholic Church] to demand some kind of "restoration and regeneration" as necessary for her existence and growth—as if it were possible for her to be subject to defect, to decay, or other such deficiencies.[1]

Forgetting the Gospel saying "Whoever is not against you is for you" (Luke 9:50), and remembering only the other saying, "Whoever is not for me is against me" (Luke 11:23), Gregory XVI saw the world around him as full of evil men attacking the Church he was leading:

> Brazen immorality, impudent knowledge, dissolute license abound. Holy things are despised, and the majesty of divine worship, which possesses both great power and great necessity, is attacked and polluted by malevolent men, and made a matter of ridicule. Correct doctrine is perverted, and errors of all kinds are insolently disseminated. Neither the Church's laws, rights, institutions, nor the holiest matters of discipline are safe from the audacity of men speaking evil . . . in an abominable manner, the schools disseminate monstrous opinions, by which the Catholic faith is no longer impugned occultly and stealthily, but horrific and deadly war is waged against it openly and everywhere. Through the instruction and example of teachers, after the minds of the youth have been corrupted, immense harm to religion and unutterable immorality has resulted.

There was no softening of language whatsoever by Gregory. He was convinced that evil was indeed abroad in the world and the Holy Catholic Church was the main target of these incredibly perverted, evil men and their organizations:

> This accumulation of misfortunes must be sought in the first place in the malice and bad will of those societies into which

whatever is sacrilegious, opprobrious, and blasphemous in the various heresies and criminal sects has flowed as if into a sewer, full of all uncleanness. These things, venerable brethren, and many others besides, perhaps even graver, which it would take too long at this time to enumerate (and which you already know), beset us with excruciating and unceasing pain.[2]

It seems that the tendency to see all difference of position as due to evil-mindedness comes easily to holders of the papacy. The same kind of really quite vicious language is found in Gregory's successor Pius IX. In 1864 he issued the encyclical *Quanta cura* with a Syllabus of Errors. In it he wrote:

These persons do not hesitate to assert that "the best condition of human society is that wherein no duty is recognized by the Government of correcting by enacted penalties the violators of the Catholic religion." . . . From this totally false notion of social government, they fear not to uphold that erroneous opinion most pernicious to the Catholic Church. . . . called by our predecessor, Gregory XVI, "madness" [*deliramentum*], namely, that "liberty of conscience and of worship is the right of every man."

And to make certain that it was clear he was exercising his full condemnatory powers on the errors listed in this document, he concluded:

Therefore do we, by our apostolic authority, reprobate, denounce, and condemn generally and particularly all the evil opinions and doctrines specially mentioned this letter, and we wish and command that they be held as reprobated, denounced, and condemned by all the children of the Catholic Church.[3]

Again Pius X, addressing a consistory naming new cardinals early in 1907, used the occasion to speak of "rebels who profess and in cunning ways spread monstrous errors. . . . which is not a heresy but the poisonous sum-total of all heresies. . . . and seeks to destroy

Christianity."[4] Later that same year he issued an encyclical against what he called "Modernism," *Pascendi dominici gregis,* in which he wrote of

> the poisonous doctrines taught by the enemies of the Church.
> . . . there is no part of Catholic truth which they leave un-
> touched, none that they do not strive to corrupt. Further, none
> is more skillful, none more astute then they, in the employment
> of a thousand noxious devices; for they play the double part of
> rationalist and Catholic, and this so craftily that they easily
> lead the unwary into error; and as audacity is their chief char-
> acteristic, there is no conclusion of any kind from which they
> shrink or which they do not thrust forward with pertinacity
> and assurance.[5]

To return to Gregory XVI, did Enlightenment Catholics fall into the category of "malevolent men" for the Pope (and like-minded lesser clerics)? Church historians have usually interpreted this encyclical *Mirari vos* as primarily aimed at Felicite de Lamennais and his reforming Catholic followers in France, and doubtless part of it was so oriented, especially the condemnation of the separation of Church and state. But significant portions of it were obviously composed with Enlightenment Catholicism in mind as well, and in some instances exclusively. The references above about despising holy things and attacking and ridiculing the majesty of divine worship were clearly aimed (and almost exclusively) at the liturgical reforms outlined in this writing. So too the statements about schools disseminating monstrous opinions and teachers giving corrupting examples were directed, even if not exclusively, at the wide penetration of Enlightenment reform ideas throughout much of the school system, including the universities in Catholic Germany, that has been only briefly described in these pages. In addition, *Mirari vos* contains a long paragraph condemning efforts at allowing divorce in failed marriages, in which efforts many Enlightenment Catholics shared.

One of the goals of Enlightenment Catholicism—again, mentioned only briefly in this study—was the elimination of mandatory celibacy for priests. The movement reached large public proportions in southwestern Germany at the time of the encyclical and was clearly aimed at directly by Gregory XVI:

> At this point we desire to call upon your constancy for holy religion against the vile attack on clerical celibacy. You know that it is growing by the day, thanks to the collusion of the most depraved philosophers of our time and some of the ecclesiastical orders who, unmindful of their person and their duty, are borne away by the allurements of pleasure. They have gone so far as to dare to direct public and, in some places, repeated demands to the rulers of the abolition of that most sacred point of discipline. But we are ashamed to speak at length of these base attempts.[6]

Still another charge pointed directly, and just about solely, at the reform movement in Germany was what today would be called ecumenism, but by the Pope was labeled "indifferentism":

> And now we must mention another fruitful cause of evil by which the Church is afflicted at present, namely, indifferentism —or that vicious manner of thinking, which mushrooms on all sides owing to the wiles of malicious men and which holds that the soul's eternal salvation can be obtained by the profession of any faith, provided a man's morals are good and decent.[7]

From that position it was but an easy step to the suppression of the freedom of thought and speech:

> Now from this evil-smelling spring of indifferentism flows the erroneous and absurd opinion—or rather, madness [*deliramentum*]— that freedom of conscience must be asserted and vindicated for everyone. This most pestilential error opens the door to the complete and immoderate liberty of opinions, which works such widespread harm both in Church and state. . . . Thence proceeds

transformation of minds, corruption of youth, a contempt among the people for the Church, for sacred things and laws. In one word, that pestilence is more threatening to the public weal than any other, since as experience shows, or as is known from antiquity, kingdoms which flourished by reason of wealth, of rule, and of glory perished because of this sole evil: the immoderate liberty of opinions, license of speech, and the penchant for novelties.[8]

This condemnation of freedom of thought and speech doubtless struck other reform-minded Catholics than those in Germany, but obviously also included them in a central way. So too did the condemnation of the freedom of the press, for as often seen in the above pages, Catholic Germany was full of reform-oriented books, newspapers, journals, and pamphlets:

Here reference must be made that deleterious liberty, which can never be execrated and detested sufficiently, of printing and of publishing writings of every kind, which some dare to demand and to promote with such insolence. We are struck with horror, venerable brethren, when we see with what portentous errors we are oppressed. They are spread far and wide by a multitude of books, pamphlets, and other writings, small indeed in size but very great in malice, from which comes that curse spread across the earth that we bewail.[9]

Bearing in mind that Gregory's reign from 1830 to 1846 was followed by Pius IX's from 1846 to 1878 (Pius IX repeated all these condemnations of Gregory's in his 1864 Syllabus of Errors, in which he finally condemned this proposition: "The Roman Pontiff can, and ought to, reconcile himself to, and agree with, progress, liberalism, and modern civilization,"),[10] it is quite credible that opponents of Enlightenment Catholicism could have launched an indiscriminate and obliterating attack on it. The conspiracy mentality which sees things totally in black and white needs little justification in facts to issue blanket condemnations. If that was true of these two popes, it was a fortiori also true of their likeminded followers.

NOTES

1. *Mirari vos*, August 15, 1832, in *Acta Gregorii Papae* (Roma, 1901), vol, I, pp. 169–74. All citations here are taken from the English translation by Gregory Roettger in Colman J. Barry, ed., *Readings in Church History* (Westminster, Md.: Newman: Christian Classics, 1985), vol. III, p. 40.

2. Ibid., p. 38.

3. Quoted in Leonard Swidler, *Freedom in the Church* (Dayton, Oh.: Pflaum Press, 1969), pp. 89 ff.

4. Quoted in Michele Ranchetti, tr. Isabel Quigly, *The Catholic Modernists* (London: Oxford University Press, 1969), p. 218.

5. Pius IX, *Pascendi dominici gregis*, (1907), *Acta Apostolicae Sedis*, 40 (Vatican, 1907), 594 ff.

6. Ibid., p. 40.

7. Ibid., pp. 40 ff.

8. Ibid., p. 41.

9. Ibid.

10. Ibid., p. 74.

Implications of the Demise
of Enlightenment Catholicism

$\mathcal{A}$s noted at the beginning of this study, the first task of a historian is to describe and analyze his or her subject as accurately as possible within its own time frame—even though the motivation for the particular study was in some way prompted by the historian's own cultural context. That task has been undertaken in the preceding pages. Beyond that, the historian may also properly essay other tasks, such as compare attitudes, ideas, events, etc., from two different periods. That was also done here, simply noting the similarity, or lack thereof, between Enlightenment Catholicism and Vatican II Catholicism; no attempt was made to show a causal connection between the two, for all signs pointed away from any such nexus.

But, having found an extraordinary similarity between Enlightenment Catholicism and Vatican II Catholicism, a whole series of intriguing questions present themselves to the historian, and beyond that to the theologian of today. I will analyze and comment briefly on only those questions I as historian and as contemporary theologian judge to be of most pressing importance.

First it should be noted that with all the likenesses between Enlightenment Catholicism and Vatican II Catholicism, there are also some very important differences, found mostly in theology, church-state relations, and the level of promulgation of the reforms. In contemporary Catholic theology there is not such a heavy weight placed on the role of abstract reason by itself (particularly as found in Hermesianism). Moreover, in the last nearly two hundred years there have been extraordinary advances, especially in the sense of the importance of history and symbolism, in psychology, biblical studies, and philosophical analysis, though one should not underestimate the historical research of Wessenberg nor the philosophical investigations of Bolzano (especially his four-volume *Wissenschaftslehre* in 1837).

In Church-state relations the positions of reform-minded Catholics of 1815 and 2007 are diametrically opposite. Enlightenment Catholics saw the state as one of the most effective instruments of bringing about reform within the Catholic Church because for the most part the various German states, Protestant and Catholic, were sympathetically inclined. Contemporary reform-minded Catholics, however, find the state too often an instrument of oppression or reaction (left or right) and hence have followed the banner of liberalism and French Liberal Catholicism (Lammenais and Montelambert) favoring separation of church and state.

But the most significant difference is that many of the basic reforms of the two eras were legislated on a world level, at least in principle, at Vatican II. There is no doubt that this is a massively important advance beyond Enlightenment Catholicism. It is like the difference between getting an advanced guard turned around, and getting the whole army faced in a new direction. Caution should be observed, however, since there is still a great distance to go after turning an army around, important as that is, before arriving at the destination.

The Council of Constance (1414–18) and its aftermath is proof that getting basic reform decrees passed in an Ecumenical Council and working at their implementation for a few, or even many, years does not necessarily ensure effective, lasting reform. There was a Council, reckoned as "ecumenical" by the most conservative Catholic traditionalists, which clearly declared that the Church gathered in ecumenical council was ultimately superior to the papacy (the Council proved this in deed by either persuading the then three contending popes to resign, or effectively deposing them, and then electing a new pope, Martin V). That too was a Council that decreed that from that time henceforth an ecumenical council should be held every ten years.

Yet in a few years both of these decrees were totally disregarded: there were only five Ecumenical Councils called in the next 550 years; this fifteenth-century "conciliar" period was followed first by that of the Renaissance Papacy, then the Counter-Reformation Papacy, and finally the Infallible Papacy of Vatican I—in an ever-growing absolute papal power, which deliberately attacked the reform decrees of the Council of Constance.

Another important question that is prompted by the study of Enlightenment Catholicism is why, after it had attained such extraordinary success and held so many key positions, it was almost totally obliterated in such a short time. Actually the reason is rather simple: Enlightenment Catholics were not able to accomplish a redistribution of power in the structure of the Catholic Church. This power of decision still lay almost entirely in the hands of the Pope and his curia and the bishops, who were picked by Rome. It was inevitable that a mistakenly appointed liberal bishop would die off, and be succeeded by a conservative one; the external forces temporarily restraining a conservative bishop—that is, secular politics, public opinion, etc.—would eventually shift in his favor. Then there was nothing that could protect the gains made by liberals from the conservative flood coming back in. This is what happened in the 1830s and subsequently.

The answer to this question can be put in another way, equally as simple: All final decision-making power continued to flow from the top down. For the first thousand years of Western Christianity much of the power flowed upward from below, especially exemplified in the widespread participation of priests and people in the selection of bishops.[1] But with the papal triumph in the struggle over the investiture of bishops in the eleventh century, more and more of the power flow was centered in the papacy, which gradually increased its powers of episcopal appointment. Efforts were made to reverse the tide, particularly in the conciliar movement of the early fifteenth century, which culminated in the reform Ecumenical Councils of Constance (1414–18) and Basel (1431–49); the latter ended in total failure, and the papacy reestablished its almost absolute decision-making authority. Another major attempt at reversing the flow of authority was made in the sixteenth-century Reformation. But the reformers soon found themselves outside the Catholic Church, which by way of reaction was even more firmly forced into an authoritarian decision-from-above pattern for another two centuries.

As we saw above, the movements of Gallicanism, Febronianism, and even Josephinism in the eighteenth century tried in significant, though limited, ways to reverse the flow of power at the levels of the bishops and the national churches; their attempts at limited reforms met with even less success. Enlightenment Catholicism in the first part of the nineteenth century persisted in the reform effort and had the political insight in its later stages to strive for a more democratic synodal form of church decision making, which would have fundamentally shifted the flow of power to a from-below-upward direction. A parallel effort was made in France (Lammenais and Montelambert) at the same time and even in the United States with its election of bishops by the priests and lay trusteeism.[2]

But all these movements were swamped by a flood tide of Catholic conservatism, led by two of the most authoritarian, energetic, and long-lived popes—Gregory XVI (1831–46) and Pius IX (1846–78). One more try was made at the end of the nineteenth century. It took different forms, from "Americanism" in the United States, to "democratizing priests" and what was later dubbed "Modernism" in France and England, *Reformkatholizismus* in Germany, and *Rinnovamento* in Italy. Among the many reforms advocated, and to some extent undertaken, in this set of movements were efforts to redistribute power into the hands of the laity, priests, and bishops, as well as the papacy.[3] These efforts and all reform attempts were absolutely crushed by the extremely vicious ecclesiastical terrorism initiated by the anti-modernist papal decrees *Pascendi* and *Lamentabili* and the "Oath against Modernism" in 1910 (more about this following).[4]

The pattern is clear: Reform efforts have persistently had only ephemeral value and have finally failed because a shift in the flow of power to a from-below rather than from-above direction was never effectively accomplished in a reform of the Catholic Church's power structure. The historian-theologian would have to conclude that if such a redistribution of the loci of power in the Catholic Church is not accomplished in connection with the reforms of Vatican II, *all* of those reforms are likely to evaporate, as did those of the Councils of Constance and Basel, and subsequent reform movements like Enlightenment Catholicism, which vanished even from the pages of most of our history books.

The lesson here of history is clear: Reform and renewal movements are necessarily great efforts of commitment and passion, but if their gains are not eventually translated into structural change, into *law* and practice, they will be washed away! It is only by recasting the decision-making structure of the Catholic Church away from its medieval version of the Roman Imperium (power from above) back to its more nearly democratic (power from below) structure of its first centuries, and then further forward to a truly democratic structure fitting for the twenty-first century that reform and renewal can firmly transform the Church. Hence, the Catholic Church must relinquish its imperial form of government adopted from the Roman Empire in the fourth century and adopt the democratic governance structure—and reflect that shift in its law and new basic Catholic Constitution (*Lex Fundamentalis*) that Pope Paul VI called for.[5]

NOTES

1. Peter Stockmeier, "Congregation and Episcopal Office in the Ancient Church," in *Bishops and People*, ed. & trans. by Leonard and Arlene Swidler (Philadelphia: Westminster Press, 1970), pp. 71 ff.

2. For details, see Leonard Swidler, *Toward a Catholic Constitution* (New York: Crossroads, 1996).

3. Leonard Swidler, "People, Priests, and Bishops in U.S. Catholic History," Swidler and Swidler, *Bishops and People*, pp. 113 ff.

4. Leonard Swidler, *Freedom in the Church* (Dayton, Oh.: Pflaum Press, 1969), pp. 136 ff.

5. See Swidler, *Toward a Catholic Constitution*.

II

ENLIGHTENMENT
CATHOLICISM REDIVIVUS

· 6 ·

Enlightenment Catholicism Redivivus

$\mathcal{I}$n light of the results of our previous historical research, are then all Catholics committed to Church renewal and reform condemned to either splintering or a Sisyphusan drudge? I think not. However, the key is, as noted, to change the decision-making structure to be appropriately congruent with the *Zeitgeist,* or as St. Pope John XXIII put it, following the "Signs of the times." Clearly the decision-making structure that is appropriate for the twenty-first century and subsequently is a democratic one, one which fosters the growth of the Church members as adult participants.

At the foundation of a democratic governance structure is a fundamental law, that is, a written *Constitution* which sets out the basic principles on which all subsequent laws and behavior are based. This is something that Americans, and Westerners in general, as well as vast numbers of other people around the world, are very familiar with. This is also something Pope Paul VI well understood when he called for the drafting of a Constitution for the Catholic Church in 1965. Despite this fact, many, if not most, Catholics are still chary about speaking of democracy, rights, and Constitution in the Catholic Church. I will offer below ample grounds to dispel that hesitancy, but here I would like to stress the absolute necessity of a Constitution for the Catholic Church which will assure the democratic governance structure of the Church being *written,* approved, and put into practice.

How is this to take place? Pope Paul set up a commission to work on this project, and worked on it for seventeen years, only to be summarily cashiered by his successor John Paul II in 1981. Must we then simply wait until some future pope might be similarly inspired and actually carry the project to its conclusion? That would hardly be responsible. But if I am not a highly placed cardinal, what can, should, I do about it, if anything?

My strong urging is to promote a "Constitutional Movement from Below." We need to act on the parish level to gather all the members together—pastor, religious, lay leaders, and parishioners—to go through the process of drafting a Constitution for the parish, and then live by it. From there the example will spread to other parishes, because a Constitutional parish will be a flourishing parish. Eventually the practice will jump to the diocesan level—for there is nothing in current canon law which prohibits the drafting and using of such Constitutions.

But again, more of this below. The first task to be accomplished here is to help change the *consciousness* of Catholics to understand that democracy, rights, Constitutions are all more than compatible with Catholicism; they are in fact much more in keeping with Jesus and Christianity than the present imperial-feudal system of governance we have inherited from the Roman empire and Middle Ages. Let me outline a number of steps that need to be taken in that direction, some of which have already begun.

FIRST REVIVAL OF
ENLIGHTENMENT CATHOLICISM

But even before that, a brief historical context: As seen previously, Enlightenment Catholicism was resisted viciously by Rome, which succeeded in removing Ignaz von Wessenberg from administrative power in the early 1830s, drove a further nail in its coffin with the wide failure of the 1848 republican revolutions across Europe, and seemingly finally laid it to rest with Pius IX and his *Syllabus of Errors* (1864) and the Vatican Council I declaration of papal infallibility (1870).

However, in 1878 Pius was replaced by Pope Leo XIII (1878–1903). Leo was by no means a liberal (as a cardinal he even encouraged the *Syllabus of Errors!*), but in comparison to his two also long-lived predecessors, Gregory XVI (1832–46) and Pius IX (1846–78), he must have seemed so. Gregory and Pius were both violently opposed to democracy, and when the thousand-year-old Papal States were seized by the newly formed Italian nation in 1870, Pius already had in place his preemptive *"non expedit"* policy (1868), that is, it was "not expedient" for Catholics in Italy to participate in the burgeoning Italian democracy by voting and the like. In France, 1870 brought the German defeat of Emperor Louis Napoleon and the horrors of the year-long Paris Commune with its anti-clerical violence—reminiscent of the 1790s Jacobin Reign of Terror. Understandably, the Church supported monarchist causes rather than republican, so that when the republic was established in 1871 anti-clericalism was its watchword (*le cléricalisme, voilà l'ennemi!*). Unlike Pius, Leo eventually (really "too little, too late") launched a policy of support of the French Third Republic in 1892 known as *Ralliement* ("rallying" to the republic).

From the time of the sixteenth-century Reformation, the Catholic Church in its effort to combat the Protestant stress on the free interpretation of the Bible by every layperson had felt forced to place stringent limitations on the reading of the Bible. By the time of Leo XIII, however, there was an increasing Catholic emphasis on the use of the Bible so that in his 1893 encyclical *Providentissiums Deus* Leo encouraged Catholic biblical scholarship, insisted on strengthening the biblical training of the clergy, and even granted an indulgence for the regular reading of Scriptures![1] In the *Constitutio officiorum ac munerum* of January 25, 1897, the publishing of the original texts of the old Catholic translations of the

Eastern Church was approved, and all limitations on possessing and reading approved translations of the Scriptures were set aside; from this document the canons on Scripture reading were developed.[2] In 1902 Leo XIII set up the "Papal Biblical Commission" as an official papal organ to *foster* biblical studies by encouragement and advice—but which, unfortunately, under Pius X became a restrictive instrument. Leo also laid plans for the founding of an institute for biblical studies in Rome; the project was only carried out by his successor Pius X in 1909, when the "Papal Bible Institute" was founded. Also in 1902 Leo founded the St. Jerome Society, which distributed 180,000 Italian copies of the New Testament in its first year.[3]

Leo also had much more of an appreciation for history than Pius IX, and so the repressions of the latter against the premier Catholic historian of the time, Ignaz von Döllinger, in 1863, were quietly dropped by Leo, but too late for Döllinger, who had been excommunicated in 1871. Still, Catholic scholarship began to revive with scholars like the brilliant church historian Louis Duchesne (1843–1922) and the equally brilliant Scripture scholars Marie Joseph Lagrange (1855–1938), who founded in Jerusalem the École Pratique d'Études Bibliques and the *Revue Biblique,* and Alfred Loisy (1857–1940), who taught at the Institut Catholique and the College de France in Paris (he was excommunicated in 1908 in the wake of Pope Pius X's anti-Modernist heresy hunt). Already in 1891 Leo wrote on current economic matters (*Rerum novarum*), and even earlier in 1880 opened the Vatican archives for the first time to the scholars of the world.

All this encouraged Catholic creative/critical thought so that a series of International Catholic Congresses was held (as had been in Malines, Belgium, and Munich, Germany, in 1862 and 1863, before Pius IX crushed the remnants of Enlightenment and Liberal Catholicism) in Paris (1888, 1891), Brussels (1894), Fribourg (1897), and Munich (1900). Wilfrid Ward, writing in 1893, stated that Leo "had notoriously encouraged historical studies and encouraged their pursuit in the most absolutely candid and critical spirit."[4] As a result there developed reform movements:

1) F.-X. Kraus' (1840–1901) and Hermann Schell's (1850–1906) *Reformkatholizismus* in Germany;
2) Don Romolo Murri's (1870–1944) *Lega Democratica Nazionali*, and Antonio Fogazzaro's (1842–1911; his 1905 best-seller novel *Il Santo* was put on the *Index of Forbidden Books* in 1908) periodical *Il Rinnovamento* in Italy;
3) "Modernism" in France, exemplified best by Loisy and the philosopher Maurice Blondel (1861–1949);
4) "Modernism" in England, represented by George Tyrrell (1861–1909) and the anglicized Austrian Baron Friedrich von Hügel (1852–1925); and
5) "Americanism" (condemned in 1899).

"It has been argued that Modernism was a conscious attempt to resume the work of Johann Adam Möhler and the Catholic Tübingen theologians of the period 1815–1840"[5]—in other words, Enlightenment Catholicism. Conscious or not, the fin de siecle saw an Enlightenment Catholicism redivivus—at least temporarily.

"ENLIGHTENMENT" CATHOLICISM DESTROYED—AGAIN

Pope Pius X, of peasant background as distinct from Leo, who was of aristocratic background, was definitely not in favor of intellectual freedom. It was in 1907 that he launched his "Anti-Modernism Heresy Hunt," which matched Popes Gregory XVI and Pius IX in reactionary fury. Every priest was obliged to take a "loyalty oath" eschewing everything that smacked of "Modernism," as sweepingly defined in Pius X's encyclical *Pascendi*, and to ensure compliance, every diocese throughout the world had to establish a secret Vigilance Council, which received denunciations in secret and issued sweeping punishments without trial:

> We decree, therefore, that in every diocese a "Council of Vigilance" be instituted without delay. . . . [They] shall be bound to secrecy as to their deliberations and decisions, and in their functions . . . they shall watch most carefully for every trace and sign of Modernism both in publications and in teaching. . . . We entrust to the Councils of Vigilance the duty of overlooking assiduously and diligently social institutions as well as writings on social questions so that they may harbour no trace of Modernism, but obey the prescriptions of the Roman Pontiffs. . . .
>
> Anyone who in any way is found to be tainted with Modernism is to be excluded without compunction from these offices, whether of government or of teaching, and those who already occupy them are to be removed. The same policy is to be adopted towards those who openly or secretly lend countenance to Modernism . . . and to those who show a love of novelty in history, archaeology, biblical exegesis.[6]

The burgeoning Catholic thought and scholarship at the turn of the twentieth century—which to a great extent was Enlightenment Catholicism brought back and brought up to date through a deepened sense of history, though the name was eschewed—were crushed and did not begin to revive until the 1940s, when Pope Pius XII began to relax the restrictions on Scripture and liturgical scholarship.

In 1943 Pius XII wrote the encyclical *Divino afflante Spiritu*. The Protestant Danish theologian Kristen Skydsgaard noted the significant difference in the situation when Leo XIII wrote *Providentissimus Deus* and when Pius XII on its fiftieth anniversary in 1943 wrote *Divino afflante Spiritu*. Skydsgaard noted that in his time Leo XIII felt the historical-critical research needed to be de-emphasized, and moreover the occasion for writing the 1893 encyclical was a "too progressive-minded" article by a highly placed theologian. (Here Skydsgaard was referring to the much-maligned Loisy.)

In the encyclical *Divino afflante Spiritu* the tone is completely different. With a rare clarity, if also in certain points with great caution, the Pope declared himself an advocate of a historical, scientific study of the Bible. What in 1893 was "allowed" with great restraint, is here "requested" and recommended.[7]

Pius XII approved the developing "Catholic Bible Movement" and ended with the words of Jerome: "Not to know the Scriptures means not to know Christ."[8]

Thus again a more historicized Enlightenment Catholicism began to creep back, though again the name was completely forgotten. This period also saw the rise of the *Nouvelle Theologie*, a creative attempt on the part of a number of outstanding theologians (e.g., Henri de Lubac, Yves Congar, Hans Urs von Balthasar) to revive Catholicism by, among other things, going back (*ressourcement*) to the theology of the Fathers (Patristics) of the Church. This renewed Catholic thought was automatically strongly resisted in Rome, resulting in the suppressive encyclical *Humani generis* in 1950, and Catholic ecumenical efforts were likewise rebuffed by a 1948 Vatican *Monitum* and a 1949 *Instructio*.[9] Nevertheless, slow progress was made in theology, scriptural and liturgical studies, and ecumenism in the 1950s, a slow, almost sotto voce, now historicized "Enlightenment Catholicism Re-Redivivus." Then came the "cardinals' mistake"—Saint Pope John XXIII!

SAINT POPE JOHN XXIII'S *"AGGIORNAMENTO"* ENLIGHTENMENT CATHOLICISM RE-REDIVIVUS

Cardinals' mistake?

When [Cardinal Angelo Giuseppe] Roncalli was elected pope, he was expected by the Curia to be a "caretaker" or "interim" pope. There were no major crises in the Church in 1958; there were no significant heresies or controversies abroad. Roncalli was an old man [seventy-seven years old] who would fill the office of pope well if he were simply his cheerful, humble self. If he were to be true to his motto [*Oboedientia et Pax*], he would seek peace through obedience to the way things had been. Imagine their surprise when he began to speak about an ecumenical council within three months of his election.[10]

Professor George Lindbeck, a Lutheran Observer at Vatican II, pointed out the "lull" in the life of the Catholic Church at just the time that John XXIII was elected pope:

> The Council occurred in what was, in retrospect, a remarkably calm moment in the history of the Western churches. The defeat of theological liberalism [Adolf Harnack et al. for Protestantism and "Modernism" for Catholicism], the triumph of a return to the historical doctrinal commitments of the Church represented by neo-orthodoxy [preeminently by Karl Barth for Protestantism and anti-Modernism for Catholicism] and by a renewed emphasis on the Confessions in churches like the Lutheran: this was not yet being challenged at the time of the Council.[11]

Hence, it is no surprise that John XXIII saw the guidance of the Holy Spirit behind his calling Vatican Council II, remarking that he was "welcoming as from above the intimate voice of our spirit, we considered that the times now were right to offer to the Catholic Church and to the world the gift of a new Ecumenical Council."[12]

Given that Angelo Roncalli was a young priest in Italy finishing his doctorate in theology at the beginning of the twentieth century when Catholic renewal was flourishing, it is not surprising that he stood then at the edge of the circles of so-called "Modernists." Fortunately, however, he was not tarred with the brush that smeared them, and survived to one day vindicate their open and dynamic spirit as Pope.

Below I will touch briefly on the almost unknown role of American Catholicism in the framing of the 1948 United Nations Universal Declaration of Human Rights. Similarly almost unknown is the role Cardinal Roncalli played in its development:

It is noteworthy that one of those who played an important part in the formulation of the draft Universal Declaration of Human Rights was Monsignor Roncalli, as he then was, subsequently Pope John XXIII. Monsignor Roncalli was then Papal Nuncio in Paris. . . . He often, in conversations with me, expressed the hope that the Universal Declaration would save humanity from another war.

The eminent French jurist and Nobel Peace Laureate, the late René Cassin, has paid eloquent tribute to the assistance which Monsignor Roncalli then gave to the French Delegation. This may also possibly explain the fact that some fifteen years later in his encyclical *Pacem in terris,* Pope John XXIII makes specific reference to the need for a Charter of Fundamental Human Rights.[13]

My favorite photo of Pope John XXIII was in the common room of the Carmelite monastery in Washington, D.C. It showed John obviously at a party with a cigarette in one hand and a martini in the other. That goes along with one of the many stories of his sense of humor:

> While in Paris, Roncalli once said: "You know, it's rough being a papal nuncio. I get invited to these diplomatic parties where everyone stands around with a small plate of canapes trying not to look bored. Then, in walks a shapely woman in a low-cut, revealing gown, and everyone in the whole place turns around and looks—*at me!*"[14]

However, the *integristes,* the ultra-conservatives of twentieth-century European Catholicism, were not laughing just three months after he was elected pope when John, preceding Martin Luther King Jr. by a decade, uttered the words "I had a dream" before the cardinals gathered by him in Rome on January 25, 1958. He then proceeded to tell them that he had a dream of going around the Vatican opening the windows and that he was going to call an Ecumenical Council. "It was completely unexpected, like a flash of heavenly light."[15]

He wrote of learning "how to distinguish the 'signs of the time' (Matthew 16:4),"[16] and of the Church "bringing herself up to date" (his famous *aggiornamento* in Italian). He made it clear that Vatican Council II was to be positive in its tone, saying clearly that "We must disagree with those prophets of gloom, who are always forecasting disaster. . . . In the present order of things, Divine Providence is leading us to a new order of human relations." He noted that though it was important to hold fast to the good of the Tradition, "at the same time she [the Church] must ever look to the present, to the new conditions and new forms of life introduced into the modern world which have opened new avenues to the Catholic apostolate."

He added his now well-known distinction between the matter and form of doctrine:

> Authentic doctrine . . . however, should be studied and expounded through the methods of research and through the literary forms of modern thought. The substance of the ancient doctrine of the deposit of faith is one thing, and the way in which it is presented is another. And it is the latter that must be taken into great consideration with patience if necessary.[17]

Would that Pope John Paul II and Cardinal Ratzinger (later Pope Benedict XVI) kept these words more prominently in their thoughts.

One might think that there would have been an opposition between those theologians who were promoting *ressourcement* and those following John XXIII with his key word *aggiornamento*. But to so think would, as Lindbeck makes clear, be mistaken:

> The *ressourcement* and *aggiornamento* people at the Council thought of themselves as collaborators. *Ressourcement* and *aggiornamento* were understood to be two dimensions of the same reality. But the dimension labelled "*aggiornamento*" could be used in a program of accommodation to the modern world, rather than one of an opening to the modern world; and when that happened, *aggiornamento* fell into opposition to *ressourcement*. But in my memory of the Council, there was absolutely no tension between the two.[18]

POPE PAUL VI'S "NEW THINKING"

John XXIII lived through the first session of the Council and, having thus definitively launched Enlightenment Catholicism Re-Redivivus, then was followed by Cardinal Montini as Pope Paul VI, who carried the Council to its completion.

What must be borne in mind when focusing on the development of the modern moves for democratization in the Catholic Church is that it took place within what Pope Paul VI called "New Thinking."[19] (This was long before Mikhail Gorbachev in the late 1980s borrowed the phrase "New Thinking"—*glasnost* and *perestroika*—to popularize his new approach to Communism.) This "New Thinking" was characteristic of Vatican II and was likewise supposed to characterize the subsequent revision of the 1917 Code of Canon Law.

Pope John Paul II described this resultant shift in thinking, this "New Thinking" of Vatican II, in the following manner when promulgating the new Code of Canon Law (1983) for the Latin Church:

1) the Church seen as the People of God,
2) hierarchical authority understood as service,
3) the Church viewed as a communion,
4) the participation by all members in the three-fold *munera* (functions) of Christ (teaching, governing, making holy),
5) the common rights and obligations of all Catholics related to this, and
6) the Church's commitment to ecumenism.[20]

James Provost added further: "In addition to providing the basis for understanding the new canon law, these elements set an agenda for the church, an agenda which might be considered to form the basis for a kind of 'democratizing' of the church."[21]

THE TERM "DEMOCRACY"

Something must be said about the words "Constitutional" and "convention," because for many Catholics they have such a secular political, non–Catholic-Church tone about them. But even more troublesome for some Catholics is the term, and even the concept, "democracy," within whose framework "Constitution" and "convention" fall. Even the title of the relatively recent book edited by Provost and Walf is revealing: *The Tabu of Democracy within the Church*. Talk of Catholic rights, human rights in the Church, and a "Catholic Bill of Rights" also all seem to disturb a number of intelligent, informed Catholics.

But none of that unease is warranted. In a number of instances no less a stalwart of tradition than Pope John Paul II has explicitly made that clear. Pope John Paul II has advocated (1) participation in making choices which affect the life of the community, (2) a role in the selection of leaders, (3) provision for the accountability of leaders, and (4) structures for effective participation and shared responsibilities.

> The Church values the democratic system inasmuch as it ensures the participation of citizens in making political choices, guarantees to the governed the possibilities both of electing and holding accountable those who govern them, and of replacing them through peaceful means when appropriate. . . . Authentic democracy . . . requires . . . structures of participation and shared responsibility.[22]

Pope John Paul II spoke these words about democracy in civil society, but we Catholics should not shy away from contemporary democratic political terminology any more than our Catholic ancestors shied away from the imperial political terminology of their time: for an "Ecumenical (*Oikumenikos*, Universal) Council" is simply the imperial Greco-Roman political terminological equivalent of the modern democratic "Catholic (*Katholos,* Universal) Constitutional Convention." The Church did not hesitate to meet under the protection of the then-predominant civil agency, the emperor—indeed, the emperor, or empress (!), called the first seven Ecumenical Councils—that is, the first seven "Catholic Constitutional Conventions." Because democracy is a more fully human (and therefore, more fully in keeping with humanity's being the "image of God," the *imago Dei*) political structure than an empire, a fortiori we Catholics should not hesitate to meet in a democratic Ecumenical Council—that is, a Constitutional Convention.

Pope John Paul's predecessor, Pope Paul VI, as we have seen, already called for a *Catholic Constitution,* a *Lex Fundamentalis Ecclesiae.* He went further in 1967 and 1971, stating:

> It belongs to the laity, without waiting passively for orders and directives, to take the initiative . . . infuse a Christian spirit into the mentality, customs, laws, and structures of the *community in which they live.* [Paul VI, *Populorum progressio* (1967); italics added. *One of the most important communities we live in is the Catholic Church!*] Let each one examine himself, to see what he has done up to now, and what he ought to do. It is not enough to recall principles, state intentions, point to crying injustice, and utter prophetic denunciations; these words will lack real weight unless they are accompanied for each individual by a livelier awareness of personal responsibility and by effective action.[23]

This is an extraordinary papal "Call to Action" for *all.* If it is considered vital to answer it in the civil sphere, all the more so is it vital to answer it in the most important sphere of life, the Church!

Pope John Paul II continued on this path when he noted that

> Democracy . . . represents a most important topic for the new millennium . . . [the Church] values the democratic system inasmuch as it ensures the participation of citizens in making political choices, guarantees to the governed the possibility both of

electing and holding accountable those who govern them, and of replacing them."[24]

THE TERM "CONVENTION"

When one speaks of democracy, as noted, the term "constitution" comes up, and with it a constitutional convention. Some, however, have quivered with nervousness at the thought of using the more political term "convention" rather than the ecclesiastical ones, "council" or "synod." The terms "council" and "synod" have been used largely interchangeably throughout Catholic history, both meaning a meeting of persons "gathered together." "Council" is simply the Latin form, and literally means a "calling together" (*con-calare*); and "synod" is the Greek form, and literally means a "coming together" (*syn-hodos*). The term "convention" in fact is a more literal Latin translation of the earlier Greek "synod," for it also means a "coming together" (*con-ventio*). So, why not use the Latin cognate, "convention," which is closer to the earlier Greek? Vatican II itself does when referring to itself, terming itself a "*Conventus.*"[25] Also, as will be detailed in the following, for twenty years the first bishop of Charleston, South Carolina, held annual "Conventions" of his diocese, which were mandated by his "Constitution."

THE TERMS "CONSTITUTION" AND "BILL OF RIGHTS"

The term "constitution" does appear in church documents, most recently in the titles of several of the documents of Vatican II—that is, the "Constitutions" on the Church, on Revelation, etc. The term "constitution" is used because the matter treated is "constitutive" of Christianity. The term "Bill of Rights" of course does not appear in ecclesiastical documents because it is a specifically English and American phrase, but its exact equivalent does appear from the pens of both Popes Paul VI and John Paul II and long before that from the American Catholic bishops.

During Vatican Council II, on November 20, 1965, Paul VI spoke of a "common and fundamental code containing the constitutive law (*Jus Constitutivum*) of the church" which was to underlie both the Eastern and Western (Latin) codes of canon law. It was clearly what Americans refer to as a "constitution."[26] Thus was born the modern idea of a "Constitution," a *Lex Ecclesiae Fundamentalis*—more about the *Lex* shortly. In his address to the Roman ecclesiastical high court, the Rota, just one month after the promulgation of the new Code of Canon Law (1983), Pope John Paul II called specific attention to the "Bill of Rights," "*Carta Fondamentale,*" in the Code:

> The Church has always affirmed and protected the rights of the faithful. In the new code, indeed, she has promulgated them as a "Carta Fondamentale" (confer canons 208–223). She thus offers opportune judicial guarantees for protecting and safeguarding adequately the desired reciprocity between the rights and duties inscribed in the dignity of the person of the "faithful Christian."[27]

American Catholics have a major precedent for the use of the terms "Constitution" and "Convention" in that outstanding Catholic bishop of Charleston, South Carolina, from 1820 to 1842, John England. He wrote a democratic "Constitution" with which his diocese was most creatively governed. He informed Rome, writing that

> The people desire to have the Constitution printed, so that they may have a standard by which they may be guided. I have learned by experience that the genius of this nation is to have written laws at hand, and to direct all their affairs according to them. If this be done, they are easily governed. If this be refused, a long

and irremediable contention will ensue. By fixed laws and by reason much can be obtained, but they cannot be compelled to submit to authority which is not made manifest by law.

Following his "Constitution," every year a "Convention" was held to review matters and plan the coming year.[28]

Concerning the official Catholic use of the terms "Rights" and "Bills" or "Declarations of Rights," American Catholic history in the middle of this century needs to be recalled. In December of 1946, just a year and a few months after the end of the Second World War, the Administrative Board of the American Catholic Bishops' official agency, the National Catholic Welfare Conference (the Administrative Board was composed of ten bishops with Cardinals Samuel Stritch of Chicago and Francis Spellman of New York at the head), issued in the name of the American Catholic episcopate a declaration entitled "Man and Peace."

They argued that the fundamental problem of the post-war period was the understanding of what it meant to be human. They were critical of the victorious powers (mainly the USSR) for not releasing prisoners of war and for forced labor practices, and of the Western Allies for succumbing to the totalitarian pressure from the East to drive out millions of Germans from their homes. They called upon all the signatories of the United Nations Charter "to work together in the establishment and fostering of respect for human rights and the fundamental freedoms for all, without regard to race, language, or religion." They ended with a ringing commitment: "For us . . . it is impossible to remain self-satisfied and actionless while our brothers in the human family groan under tyranny and are hindered in the free exercise of their human rights."

One specific action followed immediately. In January 1947, a committee made up of laity and bishops appointed by the National Catholic Welfare Conference issued nothing less than a "Declaration of Human Rights,"[29] almost two years before the United Nations proclaimed its "Universal Declaration of Human Rights" in December 1948. In fact, the American Catholic Declaration was handed over to the Committee on Human Rights of the United Nations, the chair of which was Eleanor Roosevelt. A comparison of the American Catholic Declaration (which with fifty articles is more detailed than the UN Declaration with thirty articles) and that of the United Nations reveals amazing similarities, some passages of the latter being even verbatim copies of the former. The Catholic document speaks of human "personal dignity . . . being endowed with certain natural, inalienable rights. . . . The unity of the human race under God is not broken by geographical distance or by diversity of civilization, culture, and economy."

After the General Preamble there are four major parts, the first being "The Rights of the Human Person" (eighteen articles): "The dignity of man, created in the image of God . . . is endowed as an individual and as a member of society with rights which are inalienable," which include life; liberty; religion; equal protection of the law regardless of sex, nationality, color, or creed; information and communication; choice of state of life; and education. The other parts are the rights pertaining to the family (nine articles), domestic rights of states (ten articles), and rights of states in the international community (thirteen articles).

Here is a chapter of American Catholic history that was almost forgotten. After its initial impact,[30] no one seemed to remember or record it, until 1990.[31] And yet this is a chapter of history that makes one proud of being an American Catholic. The American Catholic Church here took the lead in promoting human rights on a worldwide basis and probably had a significant influence in the drafting of the United Nations' 1948 Universal Declaration of Human Rights.

Hence, there is ample precedent in church documents for using the terms "democracy," "rights," "bill of rights," "constitution," and "convention."

Thus, a Third Millennium international "Catholic Constitutional Convention" to decide on the fundamental constitutive structures of the Catholic Church is not a radical, new departure from tradition. Very much on the contrary. Though it is of the essence of Paul VI's and John Paul II's "New Thinking," it is also very much a return to our founding tradition, our First Millennium "Constitutional Conventions." Moreover, it should be recalled that those First Millennium "Catholic Constitutional Conventions" (Councils) not only had lay as well as clerical participants, but were even called by the then predominant lay political agency—the emperor, or empress—and were not accepted as official until promulgated by laity, the emperor/empress. Hence it is traditional and appropriate that the Third Millennium "Constitutional Convention" also have lay as well as clerical participants and be called by the now predominant lay political agency, the *Demos*, the people.

A (HALF)STEP ALREADY TAKEN

On April 24, 1994, the Plenary Assembly of the *Bund der Deutschen Katholischen Jugend* (BDKJ, "Association of German Catholic Youth," an official organization of the Catholic Church in Germany with over 500,000 members) formulated and approved a "Plan to Promote Democracy" in the Catholic Church. It was very strong, laying out in detail the current dissatisfaction among many Catholics: "For a long time there has been an increase of voices—and even precisely of the committed Christians of the Catholic Church—which have been expressing their dissatisfaction with the still dominant clericalism, centralism, and patriarchalism and demanding a change in the Church."[32] The Plan went on to claim that

> Instead of experiencing themselves as equally valuable and acknowledged partners in the Church, they time and again are treated as incompetent objects of clerical tutelage. Especially girls and women dramatically encounter the current ecclesiastical legal situation and practice in which they find themselves as

an experience of structural and personal disparagement and injustice.

Instead of trust in the liveliness of Christian groups, communities, and local churches, Christians most of the time experience the centralizing measures of an angst-filled Church which more and more values uniformity rather than variety and is suspicious of every pluralism of opinion, expression, and form of life within the Church.

The concentration of power within the Church in the hands of the clergy excludes the laity in most questions (and precisely in those which affect them) from co-responsibility and decision. A decision which provides the laity with equal possibilities in decision making is not foreseen, and in the best of cases would carry only non-binding advisory weight.

These contradictions between Church and cultural/societal reality bring more and more Christians into personal difficulties and conflicts, make their personal witness of faith and their Christian involvement in society unnecessarily more difficult, and massively endanger the credibility of the Church in general.[33]

The document then produced a number of concrete demands, including the following:

In decision-making questions of Church life the laity can participate, if at all, only in an advisory capacity. The faithful, however, are to be taken seriously as subjects of their faith, as bearers of the Church's life as *Communio* with equal rights. This, therefore, is not accomplished with the possibilities of giving advice alone without real shared working and shaping plenary power. The BDKJ demands, therefore, access to and the creation of decision-making structures in which all—including the laity—can appropriately participate:

The calling to Church offices, the ordering to Church responsibility and the staffing of leadership bodies must result from votes by the Christians concerned, which may not be restricted by a veto power by a Church officer. . . . Decisions should take place only when those concerned have been heard and have participated in the decision-making process. . . . The BDKJ demands a participation of women in all Church functions. This demand of course includes—though not only—the office of Church ordination. This presumes that the Church sets in motion a discussion of the concept of office that has prevailed until now. . . . The BDKJ demands that women participate in the formation of priests. . . .

The understanding of office which long has characterized the structure of the Church leads to a monopolizing in the hands of office holders the powers of setting norms, making decisions, and carrying them out. Church office is often law-giver, judge, and executive body all in one. This concentration of power burdens a dialogical collaboration of laity and clergy. In disputed issues a nonpartisan mediating and judging agency is lacking by way of both substantive differences and formal ambiguities. In such instances the laity lacks the possibility of calling upon an independent agency. . . . The BDKJ demands the establishment of independent arbitration and mediation agencies.[34]

The Executive Director of the BDKJ, Mr. Michael Kröselberg, in the spirit of that document took a vigorous part as a panelist, along with Professor Norbert Greinacher of the Catholic Theology Faculty of the University of Tübingen, Germany, on "A Constitution for the Catholic Church," responding to a lecture on the topic by Professor Leonard Swidler at the "Katholikentag von unten," June 30, 1994, in Dresden, Germany. Unfortunately, but not surprisingly, the German bishops did not accede to the demands of the German youth.

NOTES

1. "Bibelverbreitung im modernen Katholizismus," *Die Religion in Geschichte und Gegenwart*, vol. I (Tübingen: Mohr, 1957).

2. *Codex juris canonici* (Vatican, 1917), canons 1385, 1391, 1399, 1400.

3. "Bibellesung," *Lexikon für Theologie und Kirche* Vol. I, (Freiburg: Herder, 1957).

4. Wilfrid Ward, *William George Ward and the Catholic Revival*, p. 425, as quoted in Bernard M. G. Reardon, *Roman Catholic Modernism* (Stanford, Calif.: Stanford University Press, 1970), p. 15.

5. E. Vermeil, *Jean-Adam Möhler et l'école catholique de Tübingen. Étude sur la théologie romantique en Würtemberg et les origines germaniques du modernisme* (1913) as quoted in Reardon, ibid., p. 15.

6. *Pascendi*, Part III, sections 6, 2.

7. Kristen Skydsgaard, "Römischer Katholizismus und evangelisches Luthertum," in *Welt Luthertum von heute* (Stockholm, 1950), 310.

8. *Acta Apostolicae Sedis* 35 (1943), 326.

9. See Swidler, *Ecumenical Vanguard*, for a thorough discussion.

10. http://www.stalbg.org/misc/fortieth_anniversary_of_vatican_.htm.

11. See George Weigel, "Re-Viewing Vatican II: An Interview with George A. Lindbeck," *First Things*, 48 (December, 1994), pp. 44–50. Lindbeck explained how he came to be a Vatican II Observer: "Before the Council started, Pope John XXIII invited each of the world confessional organizations to delegate three official observers who would attend the Council. The Lutheran World Federation was one of those organizations; the United States was, in those days, the major source of funding for the LWF; so the LWF authorities in Geneva decided that they had to name an American as one of the three delegated observers. The American would have to know Latin, German, and French, would have to have had some experience of Roman Catholic theology, and, perhaps hardest of all, would have to get a leave of absence from his regular job. They scraped and scraped the barrel, and at the bottom there was an untenured Yale teacher whose dean and department were not bound by the draconian faculty employment rules now in effect. So I was named the junior member of the Lutheran delegation, and as it happened, I was the only one assigned full-time to Council business between the sessions of the Council which, as you remember, took place in the fall months of the years 1962–1965. I actually lived in Rome with my family from 1962 to 1964."

12. John XXIII, Apostolic Constitution *Humanae salutis*, November 25, 1961, convoking the Second Vatican Council sometime in 1962, in Walter

Abbot, ed., *The Documents of Vatican II* (New York: Herder and Herder, 1966), p. 705.

13. Quoted in Leonard Swidler, "Human Rights: A Historical Overview," in Hans Küng and Jürgen Moltmann, eds. *Concilium: An International Review of Theology*, 228 (1990, 2); also in French, German, Dutch, Italian, Spanish, and Portuguese editions.

14. http://elvis.rowan.edu/~kilroy/JEK/06/04.html.

15. Pope John XXIII, Opening Speech to the Council, October 11, 1962, in Abbott, *Vatican II*, p. 712.

16. *Humanae salutis*, Abbott, *Vatican II*, p. 704.

17. John XXIII, Opening Speech, Abbott, *Vatican II*, pp. 712–715.

18. Weigle, "Re-Viewing Vatican II."

19. Paul VI used the phrase *novus habitus mentis*. Paul VI, allocution of November 20, 1965, *Communicationes*, 1 (1969), pp. 38–42

20. James Provost, "Prospects for a More 'Democratized' Church," in James Provost and Knut Walf, eds., *The Tabu of Democracy within the Church, Concilium*, 1992/5 (London: SCM Press, 1992), p. 132. See John Paul II's Apostolic Constitution *Sacrae disciplinae leges*, January 25, 1983; *Acta Apostolicae Sedis*, 75/2 (1983), p. xii.

21. Provost, "Prospects."

22. John Paul II, *Centesimus annus*, no. 46 (1991); in Provost, "Prospects," p. 141.

23. Paul VI, *Octogesima adveniens* (1971).

24. "Message of the Holy Father John Paul II to the Participants in the Sixth Plenary Session of the Pontifical Academy of Social Sciences," http://www.vatican.va/holy_father/john_paul_ii/speeches/2000/jan-mar/documents/hf_jp-ii_spe_20000223_acd-sciences-plenary_en.html.

25. "Message to Humanity," issued at the beginning of the Second Vatican Council by its Fathers, with the endorsement of the Supreme Pontiff, cited in Abbott, *Vatican II*, p. 6.

26. *Acta Apostolicae Sedis*, 57 (1965), 988.

27. *Acta Apostolicae Sedis*, 75 (1983), p. 556; *Origins*, 12 (1983), p. 631.

28. See Peter Clarke, *A Free Church in a Free Society* (Greenwood, S. C.: The Attic Press, 1982).

29. "A Declaration of Human Rights. A Statement Just Drafted by a Committee Appointed by the National Catholic Welfare Conference," *The Catholic Action*, XXIX (February 1947), pp. 4ff. and 17; and "A Declaration

of Rights. Drafted by a Committee Appointed by the National Catholic Welfare Conference," *The Catholic Mind*, XLV, Nr. 1012 (April 1947), pp. 193–96. A German translation appeared in "Eine Charta der Menschenrechte. Eine Denkschrift der Katholiken Amerikas," *Die Furche*, 8 (February 1947), pp. 4ff. Both the original American and a German translation as well as an interesting analysis can be found in Gertraud Putz, *Christentum und Menschenrechte* (Innsbruck: Tyrolia Verlag, 1991), pp. 322–30, 388–97.

30. Cf. "Basic Schedule of Rights," *Commonweal*, XLV (February 14, 1947), p. 435; "NCWC on Human Rights," *The N.C.W.C. News Service*, LXXXVI (February 15, 1947), p. 538; Dies Villeneuve, "Recent Events," *Catholic World*, CLXIV (March, 1947), pp. 562ff.

31. Dr. Gertraud Putz noted how accidental and labyrinthine her discovery of the document was: "The difficult search for the English text shall not remain hidden from the reader. Through a personal contact with Professor Johannes Schwartländer of the University of Tübingen, doubtless the most knowledgeable scholar of the history of human rights, I was directed to an American human rights expert, Professor Leonard Swidler in Philadelphia. The accident that he—who at first also knew nothing of the existence of this Declaration—is married to a historian with whom he discussed the matter made it possible that she then took up the search. In a letter dated April 18, 1990, she responded to my letter and explained the difficulty in finding the Declaration, for it had no listed author under which it could be indexed. However, the fact that Professor Arlene Swidler precisely at that time was giving a course on 'American Catholic History' at Villanova University led her to search further, and she ended by writing: 'However, I am quite sure I have found the important material by paging through the significant periodicals.'" Putz, *Christentum*, p. 325.

32. *Macht teilen, Gleichheit anerkennen. Ein Demokratieförderplan für die katholische Kirche in Deutschland* (Düsseldorf: BDKJ-Bundesstelle, 1994), p. 3.

33. Ibid., p. 6.

34. Ibid., pp. 12–15.

· 7 ·

Democracy in the Catholic Church

$\mathcal{D}$emocracy cannot be just a set of procedures, but must ultimately engender and depend on an attitude, a consciousness of life, which views human life both individually and communally as based on the central human characteristics of freedom and responsibility. A lack of such a consciousness cannot be simply replaced by a set of democratic procedures, any more than there can be a concrete being consisting of just "form" but no "content." At the same time, a democratic consciousness cannot effectively express itself except through a set of effective procedures. Further, it is only through the use of such procedures over time that a democratic consciousness can be fully developed.

Humankind has painfully developed through experience a number of democratic principles and procedures which have been found either essential or in some instances at least highly beneficial for the development and expression of a democratic consciousness of human nature, of freedom and responsibility. Among many, these include prominently:

1) participation in decision making,
2) election of leaders,
3) limited term of office,
4) separation of powers,

5) open dialogue as essential to achieving mutual understanding and creative decisions,

6) equal access to positions of leadership,

7) accountability of leaders,

8) the principle of subsidiarity (i.e., a higher agency does not
do what a lower can do),

9) the right to information, and

10) due process of law.

I will deal here only briefly with the most prominent, though obviously all of them, and those not listed here as well, need to be thoroughly presented, analyzed, discussed, and acted on eventually.

CHURCH STRUCTURES IN EARLY CHRISTIANITY

How was this freedom and responsibility, this democracy, first put
into action in the history of the Church? From the earliest docu-
mentary evidence we have, the Christian Church operated with wide
participation in decision making. This was true not only of the more
free-wheeling, charismatic churches related to Paul, but also of the
more "ordered" ones. Thus we find in the Acts of the Apostles that,
for example, "the whole multitude elected Stephen" (Acts 6:5).
Again, when a large number of people in Antioch was converted to
Christianity, it was not just the Apostles or the Elders, but rather the
whole Church at Jerusalem which sent Barnabas to Antioch (Acts
11:22). Still later in the Acts of the Apostles there is the statement:
"Then it seemed good to the Apostles and Elders, with the whole
Church, to choose men from among them and send them to Antioch with Paul and Barnabas" (Acts 15:22).

In Eusebius' *History of the Church* (323 A.D.), the major source
of the immediate post-biblical history of the Church, we find Peter
not referred to as the leader or bishop of the church at Rome, either

in the first or subsequent centuries. Rather, Linus was said to be the first bishop of Rome.[1] Moreover, Peter is indirectly referred to by Eusebius as the first bishop of Antioch(!) when Ignatius of Antioch was said by Eusebius to be Peter's second successor as bishop of Antioch.[2] (Does that mean that the "Bishop of Antioch" should be the head of the Catholic Church rather than the "Bishop of Rome"?) In any case, Ignatius is the one who provides the earliest evidence of "monoepiscopacy," that is, one bishop as head of the Church in an area (a *diocese,* in imperial Rome's political terminology), which developed in some, but by no means all, areas of the Christian world at the beginning of the second century.

Ignatius does *not* refer to a bishop at Rome. Further, the *Shepherd of Hermas,* written during the second quarter of the second century, describes church leadership at Rome as a committee of presbyters. All other early documents—the New Testament Pastoral Epistles, *1 Clement, Didache, Kerygma of Peter, Apocalypse of Peter, Epistle of Barnabas,* and the *Epistle of Polycarp*—give no evidence of monoepiscopacy at Rome or anywhere else. Only Ignatius points to monoepiscopacy, and then only in Syria and Asia Minor.[3] It is only around the middle of the second century that we have clear evidence of monoepiscopacy at Rome.[4] Concerning Peter at Rome, then, there is evidence from early tradition (and the digging in recent decades under St. Peter's Basilica in Rome) that Peter died and was buried in Rome, but not that he was head of the Christian community, the Church, at Rome.

In sum, it is clear that from earliest Christianity there were various forms of community structure, from the very charismatic Pauline community at Corinth to the more presbyterally ordered community at Jerusalem. Then later, through a long period of development, the monepiscopal structure gradually arose and slowly spread, until by the end of the second century it was generally accepted and practiced. However, even the monoepiscopacy of that time and the following centuries was by no means the nearly absolutist authoritarian power center it later became. It operated much more like a limited monarchy, or just as accurately said, a limited democracy.

ELECTION OF LEADERS

The fundamental act of choice on the part of the Christian people from the initial period of monoepiscopacy and for many centuries thereafter was that of electing their own leaders, their own bishops and priests and deacons. In this, of course, they were simply continuing the same primordial custom reflected in the New Testament documents. We find corroboration in two other first-century documents, the *Didache* and *Clement of Rome's First Letter*: "You must, then, elect for yourselves bishops and deacons"[5]; bishops should be chosen "with the consent of the whole Church."[6]

Early in the third century Hippolytus made it clear that it was an "apostolic tradition," which was still practiced, for the entire local community along with its leaders to choose its own deacons, presbyters, and bishop.[7] His testimony is closely followed by that of St. Cyprian of Carthage (d. 258 A.D.), who often referred to the election of bishops by the presbyters and people. He himself was so elected and consequently made it his rule never to administer ordination without first having consulted both the clergy and the laity about the candidates: "From Cyprian to the presbyterium, deacons, and all the people, greetings! In the ordaining of clerics, most beloved brethren, it is our custom to take your advice beforehand and with common deliberations weigh the character and qualifications of each individual."[8] Cyprian also reported a similar democratic custom prevailing in the church of Rome: "Cornelius was made bishop by the . . . testimony of almost all the people, who were then present, and by the assembly of ancient priests and good men."[9]

Cyprian also bore witness to the custom of the people having the right not only to elect, but also to reject and even recall bishops: "The people themselves most especially have the power to chose worthy bishops or to reject unworthy ones."[10] Optatus, a successor to Cyprian as bishop of Carthage, attests to the continuance of the practice of electing bishops into the fourth century when he reports: "Then Caecilianus was elected by the suffrage of all the people,"[11] and over in Asia Minor the Council of Ancyra (314 A.D.) confirmed the right of election and rejection of bishops by the people.[12] Every Catholic schoolgirl and boy knows the stories of the elections of St. Ambrose as bishop of Milan and St. Augustine as bishop of Hippo (fourth and fifth centuries) by the acclamation of the people: "We elect him!" ("*Nos elegimus eum!*"). A little later Pope St. Celestine (d. 432 A.D.) said: "No one is given the episcopate uninvited. The consent and desire of the clerics, the people, and leadership are required."[13] That redoubtable Pope St. Leo the Great (d. 461 A.D.), who faced down Attila the Hun and saved Rome from being sacked, wrote: "Let him who will stand before all be elected by all."[14] These principles from the early centuries of Christian practice were reiterated in various synods until at least as late as the Council of Paris in 829 A.D.[15]

Basically the election of bishops by the clergy and people lasted until the twelfth century—over half the present span of Christianity. Even at the beginning of the United States of America, our first bishop, John Carroll, was, with the full approval of Rome, elected at least by all of the priests of the United States; he then proposed a similar election of all subsequent bishops in America—only to be blocked by Rome.[16]

The American Heritage: John Carroll

The great Catholic "Americanists" of the end of the nineteenth century —Cardinal Gibbons, Archbishop Ireland, Bishops Keane and Spalding, etc.—were by no means the first "Americanists" in the Catholic Church. Already at the beginning of the new country there stood the initial "Americanist," the first American bishop, John Carroll. John Carroll was born into a founding family of Maryland, the only English colony in the New World established by Catholics, and the first to declare and practice religious liberty. He became a Jesuit, was trained and taught for many years in Europe, until 1773, when the Jesuits were suppressed, and then returned home to America.

There he not only continued his priestly work, but also took an active part in the American Revolution (as an emissary along with Benjamin Franklin on a diplomatic mission to Catholic Canada in 1776), much as did his cousin Charles Carroll, the only Catholic signer of the 1776 Declaration of Independence. The Carrolls, including John, were very much at home in America, and John Carroll set the new church on a course that paralleled and supported what he saw as the virtues of the new nation: religious liberty, democracy, optimism.

When Rome wanted to make him the first American bishop, he insisted that all the priests of the nation elect their bishop. Rome acceded, and John Carroll was in fact elected by them. Carroll clearly wanted this tradition to continue, as is indicated in one of his letters to a fellow former Jesuit: "I wish sincerely, that Bishops may be elected, at this distance from Rome, by a select body of clergy, constituting, as it were, a Cathedral chapter."[17] Rome did subsequently grant his wish that his two coadjutor bishops be elected by all the priests of America. Unfortunately, that is where that happy practice—which of course was reflective of the ancient tradition of the Church and to some extent was still practiced then in certain European countries—was ended as far as America was concerned. Carroll had assumed it would of course continue, and made preparations accordingly—but it was blocked by Rome. Still, there the fact stands at the beginning of American history: the election of the bishop by and from among his future constituency.

Trustee System or Trusteeism?

One of the most difficult issues John Carroll had to contend with, starting even before he was made the first American bishop, was the controversy known as "trusteeism." The trustees were the laymen of a parish who corporately were responsible for the temporal matters of the congregation. The trustee issue raised not only the question of the election of the parish leaders, the pastors, but also that of serious participation in Church matters in general.

Coming from Europe, the Catholic immigrants naturally carried with them the customs of their home countries, and at the same time were influenced by the new environment. Both the old and the new pointed to the practice of the ancient principle *cujus est dare, ejus est disponere*—that is, those who contribute should have a say in the disposition of their voluntary contributions.[18] The trustees of Holy Trinity Church in Philadelphia made the point about European customs clearly when in one of their petitions to the state legislature they wrote, "In many towns in Germany, the Catholic priests are elected or chosen by the authorities of such towns. So also in France, the bishops have not the sole and absolute right of appointing pastors, which belongs more to the civil authority."[19]

Of course those trustees were correct. One articulate trustee from Philadelphia had earlier noted that the historical tradition and canon law itself provided a foundation for some form of domestic nomination of bishops. Matthew Carey was surprised to learn that in canon law there were some things "almost unknown—certainly unnoticed," about the election of bishops, noting that the code of canon law "most expressly declared, that no Bishop shall be appointed for a people unwilling to receive him—and even that those are not to be regarded as Bishops, who are not chosen by the clergy—or desired by the people."[20]

However, as the most knowledgeable scholar on trusteeism, Patrick W. Carey, has pointed out, "The new institution of the trustee system was a legitimate outgrowth of prior European Catholic customs and not a capitulation to the republican and Protestant values in American society." He went on to state that American Catholics did not simply borrow ideas and procedures from the host society, but reappropriated flexibly and creatively the

European Catholic traditions in an American context, which was the lens through which they were viewed: "Thus, the new circumstances forced them not so much to create a new sense of lay participation as to nourish and democratize traditions of lay involvement which were already rooted in their European Catholic experiences. Democratization, however, was indeed a powerful new element."[21]

The difficulties were known not as the "trustee system," but as "trusteeism." It is extremely important to keep this distinction in mind because the vast majority of American Catholic parishes in the late eighteenth and early nineteenth centuries were incorporated under the trustee system, that is, the church buildings and properties were deeded to the trustees—but only a very few experienced any conflicts. It is that grouping of relatively few conflictual situations involving trustees that is known as "trusteeism." These conflicts almost always arose because of troublesome priests—frequently wandering immigrants—whom the congregation, or a portion of it, wished to dismiss. In other words, the congregation through its trustees claimed to have a voice in the selection, and if necessary, dismissal of its pastors.

The claims of the trustees were largely accepted during the first decades of the new nation, but the few prominent "trusteeism" conflicts eventually led to a strong resistance on the part of a growing number of bishops as the early years of the nineteenth century wore on, and the entire trustee system was eventually crushed, particularly under the leadership of the archbishop of New York, John Hughes, "a forceful advocate and practitioner of episcopal absolutism," who "in the same sentence referred to the 'venerable Brethren of the clergy and the beloved Children of the laity.'"[22]

This development had a lasting traumatic effect on American Catholicism. It engendered a mentality of opposition to lay and clerical participation in the Church's administration, producing an American Catholic Church with few if any local checks on episcopal authority. "Hostile memories were passed on from generation to generation of American bishops and clergy, creating fears, even in some contemporary clergy, of recurrences of 'trusteeism.' . . . they greatly affected . . . American Catholic structures and consciousness." However, in winning, the American bishops "merely ignored, submerged, or buried the ideological issues of the conflicts and therefore did not really solve the fundamental problem involved in trusteeism." This was: to adapt a hierarchical Church "to a democratic political climate in such a way as to preserve the values of both within the Church. Thus, the problem of more widespread participation in the American church kept arising in the subsequent history of American Catholicism."[23]

What the more reflective and articulate trustees, both clerical and lay, attempted to do was to establish an ecclesiastical "quasi-democracy in American Catholicism that would acknowledge the lay trustees' . . . rights to elect pastors and bishops, and at the same time the clergy's canonical status and prerogatives. The trustees wanted to define constitutionally the relative rights and duties of people, priests, and prelates within the church."[24] In this they had significant support from the first American bishop, who even before he was bishop wrote to one group of trustees:

> Whenever parishes are established, no doubt a proper regard, and such as is suitable to our Governments, will be had to the rights of the congregation in the mode of election and presentation; and even now I shall ever pay to their wishes every deference consistent with the general welfare of Religion.

A few months later he wrote to the pastor in question: "I know and respect the legal rights of the congregation. It's as repugnant to my duty and wish, as it exceeds my power to compel them to accept and support a Clergyman, who is disagreeable to them."[25] In another instance, as Bishop Carroll wrote to the trustees of Holy Trinity Church of Philadelphia: "Let the *election* of the pastor of your new church be so settled that every danger of a tumultuous appointment be avoided as much as possible."[26]

When after two decades the American Church was divided into several dioceses, Carroll was made in 1810 the Archbishop of Baltimore. Already in 1791 he had summoned a national synod, and later as archbishop he laid plans for a national council in 1812. However, these plans were blocked by the War of 1812–14, shortly after which he died. It was clear, however, that his legacy included as a top priority governance by consensus, as befitted both the new American democracy and the ancient Church tradition. He wanted American Catholics to make their own decisions as much as possible. Already in 1785 while he was the American Prefect-Apostolic he wrote to the Vatican Secretary of State, Cardinal Antonelli: "We desire . . . that whatever can with safety to religion be granted, shall be conceded to American Catholics in ecclesiastical affairs."[27]

America was most fortunate in having at its very beginning a giant of a leader who was fully committed to both the Catholic Church and the American nation, with its principles of democracy, religious liberty, and separation of Church and state. Perhaps it would have been expecting too much to have looked for many more bishops of his stature among his successors—though one wonders whether their election rather than appointment might not in fact have much better fulfilled that expectation.

In any case, as late as the beginning of the twentieth century less than half of the bishops of the world were directly named by the pope. Thus it is only within the last century that the right of choosing our own bishops has been almost completely taken away from the priests and people—contrary to almost the whole history of the Catholic tradition, and the beginning of the American Catholic Church.

PARTICIPATORY DECISION MAKING

In the ancient Church it was not only in the election of their deacons, priests, and bishops that the laity were involved in Church decision making. Eusebius reports that already in the second century the "faithful . . . examined the new doctrines and condemned the heresy."[28] Cyprian in the third century noted that he himself often convoked councils: "*Concilio frequenter acto.*"[29] On the burning Church issues of the day he wrote to the laity: "This business should be examined in all its parts in your presence and with your counsel."[30] And again: "It is a subject which must be considered . . . with the whole body of the laity."[31] And again: "From the beginning of my episcopate I have been determined to undertake nothing . . . without gaining the assent of the people."[32] Furthermore, this custom of participatory decision making was also prevalent in the Roman Church of the time, for the Roman clergy wrote: "Thus by the collaborative counsels of bishops, presbyters, deacons, confessors, and likewise a substantial number of the laity . . . for no decree can be established which does not appear to be ratified by the consent of the plurality."[33]

Even outside the reach of the law-oriented culture of the Roman Empire the principle of participatory decision making flourished in the ancient Christian Church. For example, in the East Syrian Church the Synod of Joseph (554 A.D.) stated that "The patriarch must do all that he does with the advice of the community. Whatever he arranged will have all the more authority the more it is submitted for examination."[34]

It was not only on the local and regional levels that the laity were actively involved in ecclesiastical decision making; from the beginning that was also true on the Church Universal level as well. In the fourth century the great worldwide ecumenical councils began, the first of course being held in 325 at Nicaea—called and presided over by a layman, the Emperor Constantine. In fact, as noted before, all the ecumenical councils from the beginning until well into the Middle Ages were always, with one exception, called by the emperors. That one exception was Nicaea II in the eighth century, which was called by the Empress Irene! Moreover, the emperors and empress called the councils on their own authority, not necessarily with prior consultation and approval of the papacy—not even, for that matter, necessarily with the subsequent approval of the papacy. That is, the decrees of the ecumenical councils were promulgated and published by the emperor without always waiting for the approbation of the papacy.

Laity were also present at the ecumenical councils, as well as the large regional councils, such as the ones at Cyprian's Carthage in the third century, the Council of Elvira in the fourth century, and again the (fourth) Council of Toledo in the sixth century, and on down through the centuries, reaching a high point in some ways at the ecumenical councils of Constance and Basel in the first half of the fifteenth century. Even at the sixteenth-century Council of Trent, laity were present and active. Only with the First Vatican Council in 1870 did the participation of the laity in ecumenical councils shrivel to almost nothing.

The American Heritage: John England—"Apostle to Democracy"

There was only one other giant church leader in America following upon John Carroll's demise in 1815 until the latter part of the nineteenth century when the subsequently "condemned" Americanists arrived on the scene. That giant was John England of Cork, Ireland, who, in 1820, was named by Rome bishop of Charleston, South Carolina. In the matter of a Catholic Constitution he merits special attention.

John England was called by his first biographer "Apostle of Democracy."[35] England was indeed a fervent admirer of democracy, but more importantly, he was also a committed and skilled practitioner of democracy in all aspects of his life, and especially as bishop. In the matter of the selection of bishops he followed in the footsteps of his great predecessor, John Carroll, in his dissatisfaction with the cabalistic appointment of American bishops by Rome. He was so frustrated in the matter that at the point when both the important sees of Boston and New York were vacant and all sorts of power brokering was in process he took the extraordinary step of placing a notice in his weekly diocesan newspaper:

To the Roman Catholic Clergy and Laity of the United States

The Sees of Boston and New York are now vacant, or if Prelates have been appointed for them, I am not aware of who they are. They will both be filled before I shall probably address you upon the necessity of having some permanent and known mode of having our Sees filled, not by faction, intrigue, or accident but in a manner more likely to be useful and satisfactory than that which is now in operation. [His plea is equally pertinent—and unfulfilled—today.][36]

England took extraordinary steps in making his diocese a model of American, and Catholic, democracy, but to appreciate them fully these steps must be seen against the background of the chaos and near schism that he walked into in the Charleston of 1820.

As noted above, American Catholic Church historiography has been marred much more by the specter than the reality of "trusteeism," which ever since has been used by bishops as a club to keep laity in submission. Recall: The laws of the new nation required that church property be placed in the possession of a lay corporation; in the early American Catholic churches this corporation was known as the trustees, and it operated much as was already the case in French Canada at that time. For the great majority of cases this system worked very well, but in a small minority of cases, partly because of a few manipulative, malcontent Irish priests and partly because of some poor administrative tactics by several of the bishops, cases of serious open conflict between the bishop and the trustees of certain churches developed—in one case a young lawyer named Abraham Lincoln defended the trustees. Because of their notoriety these few cases attained more importance than they intrinsically merited, and the fumbling of the bishops only tended to exacerbate the problems.

Charleston of 1820 was the scene of one of the longest and most bitter of these trustee conflicts. One might have expected that this situation would have forced a vigorous young bishop from outside of America to make authoritarian kinds of moves. Nothing, however, could have been farther from the truth with Bishop John England. His initial, and subsequent, actions were the very epitome of toleration, democracy, and voluntarism. "For England, the evils of trusteeism were the result of the failure of proper constitutional provisions in the original trustee charters. . . . England responded to the sources of these evils by creating his constitutional form of government."[37]

There were even precedents even in American Catholic history preparing the way for Bishop England's idea of a Constitution for the Catholic Church. Already in 1783, just ten years after the Jesuit Society was suppressed by the Pope, the then Father John Carroll, a former Jesuit, prompted initially by concern for the properties of the suppressed Jesuit Society, formed a "Constitution for the Clergy," providing a number of checks and balances concerning the use of properties, reflecting republican ideals.[38]

In addition, among some of the more reflective, knowledgeable trustees there grew the notion that "clearly defined and published rights and duties within the church would avoid capriciousness in the exercise of ecclesiastical authority. Bishops and clergy . . . should govern by written law and by reason, not by will power."[39] Nevertheless few trustees actually put forward any concrete proposals for such written regulations or constitutions. The trustees of Norfolk, Virginia, were among those few. In 1817 they sent a delegate to Rome with a plan for a "Supreme Ecclesiastical Synodus" which should manage the affairs of the new diocese of Virginia. "The plan outlined in detail the rights and duties of people, priests, and bishop in the new diocese, giving lay trustees significant powers on the diocesan as well as congregational levels of ecclesiastical government."[40]

(i) The Constitution As the first bishop of Charleston, however, John England was in a position not simply to propose, but to

act, and he did just that. To begin with, he wrote a Constitution by which his vast mission diocese (comprising the states of North and South Carolina and Georgia with perhaps only a thousand Catholics) was to be governed—a most extraordinary procedure, to say the least, especially in the time of the tide of reaction after the ebbing of the French Revolution and the defeat of Napoleon. He wrote that he had carefully studied the American Constitution, as well as other writings on the subject, and the laws and tradition of the Catholic Church, and was persuaded that his Constitution was in the best spirit of both Americanism and Catholicism. Just two years after he arrived in America he wrote to Cardinal Fontana in Rome when sending him a copy of his Constitution:

> Having paid great attention to the state of several Churches in America, and studied as deeply as I could the character of the government and the people, and the circumstances of my own flock, as well as the Canons and usages of the Roman Catholic Church, and having advised with religious men and Clergymen, and lawyers, I this day . . . published the Constitution by which the Roman Catholic Church under my charge is to be regulated, and I trust with the blessing of Heaven much disputation and Infidelity restrained. It was subscribed by the Clergy and by many well disposed Laymen.[41]

Only a few weeks after his arrival in Charleston and a strenuous pastoral journey through much of his mammoth diocese (twice the size of all Ireland), he wrote in his first Pastoral Letter: "And we ourselves have for a long time admired the excellence of your [American] Constitution."[42] Three years later, in 1824, writing to Rome, he stressed the importance of written laws in America and hence their importance for the healthy governance of American Catholicism:

> But the people desire to have the Constitution printed, so that they may have a standard by which they may be guided. I have learned by experience that the genius of this nation is to have

written laws at hand, and to direct all their affairs according to them. If this be done, they are easily governed. If this be refused, a long and irremediable contention will ensue. By fixed laws and by reason much can be obtained, but they cannot be compelled to submit to authority which is not made manifest by law.[43]

(It should be remembered that this published Constitution—in the English vernacular—preceded by almost a hundred years the first publishing of a Code of Canon Law, in 1917, still in Latin.)

The Constitution laid out the rights and responsibilities of the several parties involved in the diocese: the laity, the clergy, the bishop. Moreover, the Constitution was not simply unilaterally declared in force by England. Rather, it was submitted for acceptance to every priest and all the leading laymen of the parishes for voluntary adoption; each new congregation, as it was formed, adopted it voluntarily. In fact, St. Mary's Church, the oldest church in the diocese and the one that had previously been involved in the bitter trustee dispute with Archbishop Maréchal of Baltimore, did not accept the Constitution until 1829, at which time their representatives at the annual Convention were warmly received. Until then, England was careful to let them make up their own minds. Furthermore, the Constitution itself included a procedure for emendation.

Although, with the single exception of St. Mary's, England's Constitution quickly gained warm acceptance by his laity and clergy, it met with a very cold response by the other American bishops. At the First American Provincial Council of Baltimore, in 1829, which all the American bishops attended, it was rejected as unacceptable in the other dioceses; it was stated merely that "by this decree we do not desire to interfere with the method which the Bishop of Charleston now follows in his diocese."[44] Indeed, England's Constitution stood in the way of his being recommended for the much more populous and important sees of Boston or New York.

Bishop Patrick Kenrick of Philadelphia magnanimously wrote to Cardinal Cullen in Rome, in 1834, after the Second Provincial Council of Baltimore, that England was

> perfectly disgusted at the treatment he received at the last Council. . . . Charleston diocese is not a fit theatre for a man of his splendid talents . . . I would at any moment resign my mitre to make place for him. This I authorize you to communicate to the Sacred Congr. . . . I had proposed him for the administration of New York which most sadly needs an efficient Prelate, and in consequence of the entire unwillingness of Bp. Dubois I had offered my place in case I should be forced to put on the thorny crown of that diocese. The Archbishop had signified assent, provided the Constitution would be left behind; but now that hope vanishes.[45]

Somewhat earlier England and his Constitution had suffered the venom of the poison pen of Kenrick's predecessor, Bishop Conwell of Philadelphia, who Father Andrew Greeley in his brilliant book *The Catholic Experience* says was "In the process of making a complete fool of himself." He nevertheless had time to warn the Holy See that "if this constitution or democratic method of ruling the Church be approved by the Holy See, it might become necessary to extend it to all the dioceses here; it would mean the quick collapse of the American Church."

Greeley added: "It never occurred to Conwell that such a democratic method might have saved his diocese from utter chaos. Later he wrote to Rome warning them once again that England was violating the most sacred of ecclesiastical traditions and was threatening the American Church with ruin."[46]

England was convinced that despite the trustees' difficulties, it was far better that the Church and its clergy depend primarily on the Catholic people at large rather than the government—as it still is in many European countries, such as Germany. According to his Constitution each congregation elected representatives who were to constitute a Vestry. Then, also despite the trustee controversies, the Constitution provided that "the churches, cemeteries, lands, houses, funds, or other property belonging to any particular district [here meaning parish], shall be made the property of the Vestry of that district, in trust for the same." All money belonging to the congregation could be "expended only by authority of an act of the Vestry of that district." At the same time the approval of the bishop was also required for the sale of any property. Thus, the key notions of the American Constitution of "election of representatives," "separation of powers," and "checks and balances" were here incorporated into England's Constitution. In addition, the salary of the parish priest was also to be raised by the Vestry, but kept separate from the general funds so that no improper pressure could be levied on the Pastor. The wisdom and practicality of this structure was demonstrated by the fact that it operated flawlessly for the twenty years of England's episcopacy.[47]

(ii) Annual Convention   A second critical element of the Constitution was the provision for annual diocesan Conventions for all the clergy, and a proportional representation of the laity from each congregation elected by all the people. The Convention possessed certain decision-making powers parallel to those of each Vestry, such as control of the General Diocesan Fund (used for the seminary, schools, hospitals—all of which England started—widows and orphans and similar concerns). The bishop was required to make a full report on the expending of all funds to the Convention; England in fact did an exemplary job of this at every Convention. In addition, he took the opportunity to present an overview of the Church in all America as well as in his diocese at each Convention. Consequently his twenty-six Convention Addresses give a history of the Catholic Church in America for those years. Most importantly, it was through the Convention that the scattered Catholic churches began to grow together with a sense of unity and belonging to a larger church, a "catholic" Church, which was their Church where they had both rights and responsibilities.

In the beginning years of his episcopate the Convention was legally incorporated in each of the three states and met accordingly. It was only in 1839 that the mission diocese had developed sufficiently to legally incorporate the Convention for all three states together so that there could be a single annual diocesan-wide Convention (twenty-six state Conventions were held between 1823 and 1839). The first General Convention of the diocese lasted for seven days, with sixteen priests and thirty laymen present as delegates; in 1840 there were almost double that number. The third Convention was scheduled for late in 1841, but was delayed because of England's extended mission in Europe. Then, early in 1842, he died, and with him his Convention, Constitution, and mostly everything else, it seemed, that made him great, for the small leaders who came after him could not match the stride of his footsteps.

(iii) American Councils   Dialogue and democracy on the national level were also major concerns of England from the very beginning of his time in America. Although Archbishop Carroll had scheduled a first national Provincial Council of all the American bishops already in 1812, he was, as noted above, prevented from carrying that plan out first by war and then death. His second successor, Maréchal (Carroll's first successor, Ambrose Neale, outlived him only a little over a year), a French prelate, who perhaps somewhat understandably (remembering the French Revolution) was not enthusiastic about procedures which smacked of "democracy," did not see fit to call a Provincial Council. England wrote him often, urging the many good reasons for an immediate convocation of the Council—including the requirement by the Council of Trent that they be held every three years—but on the back of each of these letters of England's that are in the Baltimore archives there is the single word written in Maréchal's hand: "Negative."

Hence, it was only after Maréchal's demise that England was able to persuade his successor, Whitfield, to call the first American Provincial Council in 1829. It is clear from records that England dominated this Council, and all the rest during his lifetime (four altogether). He was asked to write all the Pastoral Letters (five) coming out of each of the Councils, which he did with his customary talent.

For example, concerning the first Pastoral Letter, which was on the clergy (a second one was on the laity), the premier American Catholic Church historian of the early twentieth century, Peter Guilday, wrote in 1923: "The Pastoral stands today, as it did then, as one of the clearest mirrors of priestly zeal and devotion in the English language."[48] Difficult though these Provincial Councils often were, they nevertheless did resolve many pressing problems of a growing American Church, whose population and geographical expanse were exploding, in effective collegial fashion, operating in a land that insisted on religious liberty, democracy, and separation of Church and state—all neuralgic Catholic issues during the time of Popes Gregory XVI (1831–46) and Pius XI (1846–78). Moreover, the work of these Councils, of which Bishop England has been called the "Father,"[49] had wide influence in world Catholicism. Theodore Maynard wrote that these Councils, "through their inclusion in the collection published at Maria Laach [1875], have had a remarkable influence on conciliar legislation and Catholic life throughout the world."[50] Just eight years after the death of England, Bishop Kenrick of Philadelphia wrote: "The Church in this country owes to Bishop England the celebration of the Provincial Councils, which have given form and consistency to the hierarchy and order to her internal economy."[51]

It was precisely England's strengths, however, that were his undoing with his fellow bishops. He could not get Archbishop Whitfield to call the second Council, but was able nevertheless to persuade Rome to insist on it to Whitfield—which fact doubtless galled the latter. After the Second Provincial Council, in 1834, Kenrick wrote to Cardinal Cullen:

> Little was done in consequence of the suspicion with which every measure emanating from Bishop England was viewed. The

prelates for the most part second the archbishop who felt morti-
fied that he had been obliged by the influence of Bishop England
to call the council. . . . The talents, learning, fame, eloquence of
Bishop England rendered him not an object of envy for I believe
the good prelates superior to this narrow passion but fear for they
dreaded lest his active mind and liberal views might lead them
into the adoption of measures which might weaken their authority and disturb the repose of the Church. To me they appeared to
fear where there was no cause for fear. Their votes could always
outweigh his arguments. Had they manifested a respect for his
judgment, a disposition to hear his reasons, and to adopt his suggestions if found correct, had there been more personal courtesy,
fraternal charity . . . the results of the council would have been
more consolatory. We would have not seen . . . a young man having no experience of the ministry save that which he would have
had within the college walls [Eccleston] raised to the office of
coadjutor to the archbishop.[52]

Andrew Greeley commented that the bishops led by Archbishop
Whitfield

were more eager to block John England than they were to govern the American Church, so eager in fact that they selected a
thirty-one-year-old coadjutor for Whitfield, to lessen so far as
they could the possibility that Rome might be remotely tempted
to make England the Archbishop of Baltimore.[53]

What a different course American Catholic history might have
taken had England had the personal ambition to circumvent the ca-
bal to make the disastrously incompetent Eccleston the archbishop
and had eventually ended there himself. Unfortunately for the
Catholic Church he did not; he promptly rose at the Council and
approved the nomination of Eccleston as co-adjutor of Whitfield at
Baltimore.

(iv) Deliberation and Dissent   In many ways England made it
abundantly clear that American Catholics felt—and he obviously

agreed with them—that they ought to be consulted in all important matters, including Church matters. He wrote to Rome that "The American people are a law-abiding people, and the laws are respected so long as the voice of the people is heard in their making." He reported elsewhere that the American Catholic "will never be reconciled to the practice of the bishop, and oftentimes of the priest alone, giving orders without assigning reasons for the same." He told his 1827 Convention that he was searching for and training clergy who were "attached to our republican institutions."[54]

England recognized that there could still be disagreements with Church authorities and spoke of "dissent" in a letter to U.S. Secretary of State John Forsythe in 1841 wherein he wrote that if the American bishops had found in a papal Apostolic Letter "anything contrary to their judgment, respecting faith or morals, it would have been their duty to have respectfully sent their statement of such differences to the Holy See, together with their reasons for such dissent." He even went so far, when addressing a joint session of the U.S. president (John Quincy Adams), Supreme Court, Senate, and House of Representatives in 1826, as to say:

> A political difficulty has been sometimes raised here. If this infallible tribunal which you [Catholics] profess yourselves bound to obey should command you to overturn our government, and to tell you that it is the will of God to have it modelled anew, will you be bound to obey it? And how then can we consider those men to be good citizens, who profess to owe obedience to a foreign authority, to an authority not recognized in our constitution, to an authority which has excommunicated and deposed sovereigns, and which has absolved subjects and citizens from their bond of allegiance?
>
> Our answer to this is extremely simple and very plain; it is that we would not be bound to obey it, that we recognize no such authority. I would not allow to the Pope, or to any bishop of our church, outside this Union, the smallest interference with the

humblest vote at our most insignificant balloting box. He has no right to such interference.[55]

Strong words in such a public forum in a period when reaction, not liberty, was in vogue with the papacy, as, for example, when Catholic Polish freedom fighters were condemned and handed over to the tender mercies of the Orthodox Czar by the Pope (1830), and again the Catholic Hungarians in 1848.

In summary, it is clear that for responsible dissent, for a Catholic Constitution, for democratic Catholic Conventions, for National Councils in the Catholic Church—in short, for the employment of participatory decision making, of democracy as it flows from the American civil experience in the life of the Catholic Church—Bishop John England of Charleston, South Carolina, provides a premier precedent.

The decades-long actions of the "Americanists" at the beginning of the nineteenth century were again vigorously articulated, especially by the most prominent of the "Americanists" at the end of that century, Archbishop John Ireland of St. Paul, Minnesota:

> This is an age of liberty, civil and political; it is the age of democracy! . . . The Catholic Church, I am sure, has no fear of democracy, this flowering of her own most sacred principles of the equality, fraternity, and liberty of all men, in Christ and through Christ. These principles are found upon every page of the Gospel. . . . I say that the government of the people, by the people, and for the people, is, more than any other, the polity under which the Catholic Church, the church of the people, breathes air most congenial to her mind and heart."[56]

NOTES

1. Eusebius, *History of the Church*, 3, 2.
2. Ibid., 3, 36.

3. Cf. T. Patrick, Burke, "The Monarchical Episcopate at the End of the First Century," *Journal of Ecumenical Studies*, 11 (1970), pp. 499–518.

4. Eusebius' account of the Easter controversy describes Anicetus in a monepiscopal role in Rome shortly before the death of Polycarp in 155 C.E. *History of the Church*, 4.22.1–3. Cf. James F. McCue, "The Roman Primacy in the Patristic Era. The Beginnings through Nicea," in Paul Empie and T. Austin Murphy, eds., *Papal Primacy and the Universal Church. Lutherans and Catholics in Dialogue V* (Minneapolis: Augsburg, 1974), pp. 44–72.

5. *Didache*, 15:1–2.

6. *1 Clement*, 44, 5.

7. Hippolytus, *Traditio Apostolica*, 2, 7, 8.

8. Jacques-Paul Migne, *Patrologia Latina*, 4, 317–18. "Cyprianus presbyterio et diaconibus et plebi universae salutem. In ordinationibus clericis, fratres charissimi, solemus vos ante consulere, et mores ac merita singulorum communi consilia ponderare."

9. Ibid., 3, 796–97.

10. Cyprian, *Epistle*, 67, 3, *Corpus scriptorum ecclesiasticorum Latinorum* (*CSEL*), 3.2.737. "Plebs . . . ipsa maxime habeat potestatem uel eligendi dignos sacerdotes uel indignos recusandi."

11. Optatus, *CSEL*, 34.2.407. "Tunc suffragio totius populi Caecilianus elegitur et manum imponente Felice Autumnitano episcopus ordinatur."

12. Canon 18. Cf. Karl Josef von Hefele, *Conciliengeschichte*, I (Freiburg: Herder, 1873), p. 237.

13. Celestine, *Epistle*, iv, 5; *PL*, 50, 431. "Nullus invitis detur episcopus. Cleri, plebis, et ordinis, consensus ac desiderium requiratur."

14. Leo, *Epistle*, x, 4; *PL*, 54, 634. "Qui praefuturus est omnibus ab omnibus eligatur."

15. Cf. Jean Harduin, *Acta Conciliorum et Epistolae Decretales ac Constitutiones Summorum Pontificum*, IV, 1,289 ff.

16. Cf. Leonard Swidler, "People, Priests, and Bishops in U.S. Catholic History," in Swidler and Swidler, *Bishops and People*, pp. 113–135.

17. Carroll to Charles Plowden, December 22, 1791, Thomas O'Brien Hanley, ed., *The John Carroll Papers* (Notre Dame, Ind.: University of Notre Dame Press, 1976), 3 vols., vol 1, p. 548.

18. This was stated in a letter from trustee Benedict Fenwick in Charleston, South Carolina, to the then bishop of the area, Archbishop

Ambrose Maréchal of Baltimore, on August 11, 1819. Archdiocesan Archives of Baltimore, 1-O-15.

19. Quoted in Patrick W. Carey, *People, Priests, and Prelates. Ecclesiastical Democracy and the Tensions of Trusteeism* (Notre Dame, IN: University of Notre Dame Press, 1987), p. 171.

20. Mathew Carey, *Address to the Right Reverend the Bishop of Pennsylvania, the Catholic Clergy of Philadelphia, and the Congregation of St. Mary's in the City* (Philadelphia: H. C. Carey & I. Lea, 1822), p. 30.

21. Patrick Carey, *People*, p. 5.

22. Ibid., p. 224.

23. Ibid., pp. 2 ff.

24. Ibid., p. 3.

25. John Carroll to Dominick Lynch and Thomas Stoughton, January 24, 1786, Hanley, *John Carroll Papers*, vol. I, p. 203; and John Carroll to Andrew Nugent, July 18, 1786, ibid., p. 214. Concerning Father Andrew Nugent, matters became so turbulent that the trustees went to civil court in order to remove Nugent, with Carroll's obvious approval. "Thus, Nugent was removed as Pastor by use of the secular arm when recourse to the voluntary measures of ecclesiastical discipline had failed." Patrick Carey, *Priests*, p. 15.

26. Quoted in Peter Guilday, *The Life and Times of John Carroll* (New York, 1922), p. 293. Italics added.

27. Letter of John Carroll to Cardinal Antonelli, February 17, 1785, quoted in: Annabelle M. Melville, *John Carroll of Baltimore* (New York: Charles Scribners' Sons, 1955), p. 230.

28. Eusebius, *History of the Church, Patrologia Graeca*, 20, 468.

29. Cyprian, *Epistle*, xxvi.

30. Cyprian, *PL*, 4, 256–257. "Cyprianus fratribus in plebe consistentibus salutem . . . examinabuntur singula praesentibus et judicantibus vobis."

31. Cyprian, *Epistle*, liv, Quoted in Johann Baptist Hirscher, *Sympathies of the Continent*, trans. of *Die kirchlichen Zustände der Gegenwart*, 1849, by Arthur C. Coxe (Oxford, 1852), p. 123. "Singulorum tractanda ratio, non tantum cum collegis meis, sed cum plebe ipsa universa."

32. Cyprian, *PL*, 4, 234. "Quando a primordio episcopatus mei statuerim, nihil sine consilio vestro, et sine consensu plebis, mea privatim, sententia gerere."

33. Cyprian, *PL*, 4, 312. "Sic collatione consiliorum cum episcopis, presbyteris, diaconis, confessoribus pariter ac stantibus laicis facta, lapsorum

tractare rationem. . . . quoniam nec firmum decretum potest esse quod non plurimorum videbitur habuisse consensum."

34. Canon 7, in J. B. Chabot, *Synodicon Orientale* (Paris, 1902), pp. 358 ff.

35. Joseph L. O'Brien, *John England, Bishop of Charleston: Apostle to Democracy* (New York: Edward O'Toole Co., 1934).

36. Quoted in Andrew M. Greeley, *The Catholic Experience* (New York: Image Books, 1969), p. 81

37. Patrick Carey, *People*, p. 222.

38. Hanley, *John Carroll Papers*, vol. I, pp. 59–76.

39. Patrick Carey, *People*, p. 166.

40. Ibid., p. 168.

41. Quoted in Greeley, *Catholic Experience*, p. 82.

42. Sebastian Messmer, *The Works of the Right Reverend John England*, 7 vols. (Cleveland: Arthur H. Clark Co. 1908), vol. VI, p. 238.

43. *The Records of the American Church History Society of Philadelphia*, vol. VIII (1897), pp. 458f.

44. *Concilia Provincialia Baltimore habita* (Baltimore, 1851), p. 74.

45. *Records of the American Catholic Historical Society of Philadelphia*, vol. VII (1896), pp. 290, 293.

46. Greeley, *Catholic Experience*, p. 85.

47. The bulk of the Constitution is published in Patrick W. Carey, ed., *American Catholic Religious Thought* (New York: Paulist Press, 1987), pp. 73–93.

48. Peter Guilday, *Life and Times of John England, 1786–1842* (New York: The America Press, 1927), p. 131.

49. See ibid., vol. II, p. 214.

50. Theodore Maynard, *The Story of American Catholicism* (New York: Macmillan, 1954), p. 241.

51. *Brownson's Quarterly Review*, vol. L, p. 158. Cf. Peter Clark, *A Free Church in a Free Society* (Greenwood, S.C.: Attic, 1982), 131.

52. Quoted in Greeley, *Catholic Experience*, pp. 91 ff.

53. Ibid., p. 92.

54. *Records ACHSP*, vol. VIII, p. 460.

55. Messmer, *Works*, vol. VII, p. 32.

56. John Ireland, "The Church and the Age," (October 18, 1893), *The Church and Modern Society* (New York: D. H. McBride & Co., 1903), pp. 114 ff., quoted in Patrick Carey, *American Catholic Religious Thought*, pp. 183 ff.

III

PAST LESSONS,
FUTURE STRATEGY

· 8 ·

Lessons from Enlightenment Catholicism and Catholic History

VATICAN II AND AFTERMATH

Those who experienced Enlightenment Catholicism Re-Redivivus, Vatican II, and its early aftermath as adults remember the great euphoria, the sense of release, and extraordinary optimism that it loosed among Catholics, as well as very many other Christians, persons of other religions, and even persons of no religion. It seemed to us as if we were entering into a "Brave New World"—in the Shakespearean not the Huxleian sense. There then followed the "Dark Night of the Senses" when the enlivening progress of the Council began to give way to doubts in the wake of the devastating reversal of Pope Paul VI's 1968 encyclical *Humanae vitae* against artificial birth control—flying in the face of the recommendations of 90% of his own appointed Commission consisting of Cardinals, bishops, theologians, and various scientific experts.

Still, the spirit of Vatican II remained vigorous for several more years, being reflected in several National Councils held in the 1970s. But Pope Paul VI seemed to many to become more and more a Hamlet figure, hesitating between following the path of Vatican II renewal and following the dark whisperings of the "prophets of gloom" John XXIII had warned against. With the passage of time he leaned more and more toward the latter, as shown in the several attacks on Catholic reform efforts and leaders: the attacks on the

113

brilliant, energizing Dutch Catechism, on Hans Küng, on Bernard Häring, on Edward Schillebeeckx. . . .

Then with the pontificate of John Paul II Vatican II Catholicism entered into the "Dark Night of the Soul." Pope John Paul II promoted human rights in the secular sphere; indeed, he was credited with a major role in bringing down the prison of Iron Curtain Communism. However, inside the Catholic Church it was another story. Let me illustrate.

It was a bad year, 1979. It had started poorly—and was ending worse. Three a.m. on December 18, my phone rang insistently, and I eventually answered it groggily. An American theologian/ journalist in Rome, Ed Grace, said breathlessly: "The Vatican just condemned Hans Küng!"

Late in 1978 John Paul I had died just a month into his pontificate and John Paul II was elected his successor. Then the head-hunters at the Holy Office (the words "of the Inquisition" had been struck from the title earlier in the century, but apparently not from the reality) were quickly unleashed:

1. in the spring of 1979 the French theologian Jacques Pohier was silenced for his book *When I Speak of God*;
2. in July the book on sexuality by a team of four American theologians, including Ronald Modras (an initial Board member of the "Association for the Rights of Catholics in the Church"—ARCC; see below) was condemned;
3. in September the Jesuit General Pedro Arrupe was forced to send a letter to all Jesuits that they could not publicly dissent from any papal position;
4. all autumn severe accusations of heresy against Edward Schillebeeckx, one of the greatest theologians of Vatican II and afterward, were recurrently issued in drum-beat fashion; on December 13–15 Schillebeeckx was "interrogated" by the Holy Office in Rome;

5. that same month writings of Brazilian liberation theologian Leonardo Boff were "condemned" (he was later silenced);

6. on December 18 the Holy Office issued a Declaration on Hans Küng saying he "can no longer be considered a Catholic theologian."

A few hours after the call from Ed Grace I was on the phone with Father Charles Curran of the Catholic University of America and Father David Tracy of the University of Chicago. We decided to quickly issue a press a statement by U.S. Catholic theologians stating that in our collective judgment "Hans Küng was indeed a Catholic theologian." We decided to fight Rome with Roman tactics, and took a leaf from Caesar: *Omnis America in tres partes divisa est.* For the next twenty-four hours each of us got on the phone to our third of the nation, collecting signatures. As I spoke with people, time and again the refrain sounded: This can't go on; we have got to organize!

So in the next days I drew up a proposal to organize what became the Association for the Rights of Catholics in the Church (ARCC) and sent it to all interested contacts around the country. The response was overwhelmingly positive. Group meetings were held in many cities around the United States, proposals of what needed to be done were drawn up, and delegates were chosen to be sent to the Founding Convention held March 17–20, 1980, in the Alaska Hotel, Milwaukee, Wisconsin. Thirty-two (twenty-two women and ten men) met and founded ARCC to "bring about substantive change, to institutionalize a collegial and egalitarian understanding of Church in which decision making is shared and accountability is realized among Catholics of every kind."

Three delegates, Gerard Sloyan, Dolly Pomerleau, and myself, were charged at Milwaukee with coming up with a National Board of the ARCC, which we did in the next week, sitting in Gerard's living room in Philadelphia. The first meeting of the Board (consisting of between fifteen and twenty members, deliberately diverse geographically, by gender, lay and clerical, and otherwise as much as possible) occurred in October 1980, and it has met every spring and fall since. Presidents of ARCC were James Finn 1980–83; Margaret Cotroneo 1980–86; Alan Turner 1986–89; Mary Lou Hartman 1989–98; Terry Dosh 1998–2001; Mary Lou Hartman 2001–2004; Leonard Swidler 2004–present.

A wide variety of documents were developed and issued by ARCC, such as on "Dissent and Dialogue," "Parish Rights," "The Internal Forum," the "Doctrine of Reception," and the "Spirituality of Democracy," but the two major ones were the *Charter of Catholic Rights* and *A Proposed Catholic Constitution* (see appendix A in the current text).

Patrick Connor and Leonard Swidler were the co-chairs for the Charter Committee, and editors of the book. The Charter was first issued October 25, 1983. The idea for a Constitution was first proposed by Leonard Swidler at the spring 1990 Board meeting. In 1994 Leonard Swidler and James Biechler were asked by the ARCC Board to begin the process of drawing up a Proposed Catholic Constitution. It went through many versions resulting from worldwide consultation and intense work by an ARCC Constitution Committee (Leonard Swidler, Chair, William Leahy, David Efroymson, Carol Efroymson, and Pamela Monaco), and a committee of European Catholic reform organizations. The "current" version was approved by ARCC and the European Catholic reform organizations on September 19, 1998.

In the wake of the U.S. clergy sexual abuse scandal, an "International Movement for a Catholic Constitution" was launched in Boston by ARCC and joined by other Catholic reform organizations in the United States and Europe (for information on ARCC see its website at http://arcc-catholic-rights.org/).

A CONSTITUTION OF THE CATHOLIC CHURCH

In very many ways Vatican Council II (1962–65 A.D.) was a return not only to Enlightenment Catholicism, but also to the spirit and form of the first "Constitutional Conventions" (Councils) of the early Church even though the influence of the laity came only largely through the massive power of the free press.

Another of the democratizing moves Vatican Council II made was to inspire the total revision of the 1917 Code of Canon Law in the spirit of democracy and constitutionalism. Already on January 25, 1959, Pope John XXIII announced simultaneously the calling of the Second Vatican Council and the revision of the 1917 Code of Canon Law.[1] Even before Vatican II was completed work was begun on the writing of this Catholic "Constitution of Fundamental Rights," the *Lex Ecclesiae Fundamentalis*. Father James Coriden, a co-editor of the 1985 magisterial 1,150-page folio-sized *Code of Canon Law: A Text and Commentary* (commissioned by the Canon Law Society of America) and the Dean of the Catholic Theological Union of Washington, D.C., wrote that "The origins of the Code's bill of rights [the new 1983 Code of Canon Law eventually absorbed the fundamental 'rights' articles of the *Lex Ecclesiae Fundamentalis*] were not in a Constitutional Congress, but its history and development clearly reveal its truly constitutional character."[2]

As noted above, it was on November 20, 1965, that Pope Paul VI said to the *Coetus Consultorum Specialis* (Commission for the Revision of the Code of Canon Law) that the opportunity to provide a "constitution" for the Church should be seized while the 1917 code of canon law was being overhauled in the light of Vatican II. The *Coetus* was led by Cardinal Pericle Felici (an ultra-conservative) and Msgr. William Onclin (a moderate) of Louvain University. Already by the middle of 1966 the *Coetus* had a draft prepared for discussion and a revised version the following year, 1967. That year the *Coetus* drew up and submitted to the International Synod of Bishops a set of ten "principles to guide the revision of the Code" *(Principia quae diregant recognitionem Codicis)*, which were overwhelmingly approved. Three more sessions of the *Coetus* followed, and then a first formal draft was presented to the cardinals of the *Coetus* in 1969, and was relatively widely circulated, although officially still *sub secreto*. Then in 1971, the further revised draft (so-called *textus emendatus*) was sent to all the bishops, still *sub secreto*. However, it was leaked to the press and published that March 15, 1971, in the Bologna periodical *Il Regno* (the editors were all fired for their efforts).

Two things should be especially noted about the *Lex Ecclesiae Fundamentalis*: (1) It clearly was to serve as a "constitution" in the sense that it was to provide the fundamental juridical framework within which all other Church law was to be understood and applied. Like the American Constitution , if any subsequent law passed were found to be contrary to the *Lex Fundamentalis,* the subsequent law would be void. (2) The *Lex Fundamentalis* was to serve as a fundamental list of rights of the members of the Church, like the American Bill of Rights.

Concerning the first point, the explanation (*Relatio*) by Msgr. Onclin that accompanied the 1971 draft of the *Lex* stated clearly that

> since a fundamental law is required, on which all other laws in the Church will depend. . . . Laws promulgated by the supreme authority of the Church are to be understood according to the prescriptions of the *Lex Ecclesiae Fundamentalis* . . . laws promulgated by inferior ecclesiastical authority contrary to the *Lex Ecclesiae Fundamentalis* lack all power.[3]

Concerning the second point, Father Coriden wrote referring to the *Lex Fundamentalis* as key portions of it were imbedded in the 1983 Code of Canon Law:

> The bill of rights is part of the bedrock upon which is based the rest of our canonical system. . . . The *Coetus's* communication to the Episcopal Synod of 1967 described the enumeration of rights of the faithful as fulfilling one of the chief purposes of the "fundamental code."[4]

Already in 1967 the *Coetus* told the Synod of Bishops in its ten guiding principles the following:

> The principal and essential object of canon law is to define and safeguard the rights and obligations of each person toward others and toward society. . . . A very important problem is proposed to be solved in the future Code, namely how the rights of persons can be defined and safeguarded. . . . The use of power in the Church must not be arbitrary, because that is prohibited by the natural law, by divine positive law, and by ecclesiastical law. The rights of each one of Christ's faithful must be acknowledged and protected.[5]

A further aspect of the *Lex Fundamentalis* is worth noting here. As mentioned, from the inception of the *Coetus* in 1965, until the press leak in 1971, its work was all done *sub secreto*. Why it should have been so is not clear, except that that was the way things had always been done. However, after the leak Msgr. Onclin held a press conference in which he

> recalled that the draft text was only a working paper which will probably be modified in conformity with the wishes of the bishops. These, in turn, may consult priests and laymen, and the result will therefore be a truly Church-wide consultation.[6]

As Peter Hebblethwaite mentioned in his biography of Pope Paul VI, the Vatican instruction *Communio et progressio*, on the implementation of the Vatican II decree on the mass media, was issued less than two months before the *Lex* leak in *Il Regno*. It made a clear argument in favor of open government in the Catholic Church:

> The spiritual riches which are an essential attribute of the Church demand that the news she gives out of her intentions as well as her works be distinguished by integrity, truth, and openness. When ecclesiastical authorities are unwilling to give

information or are unable to do so, then rumor is unloosed and rumor is not a bearer of truth but carries dangerous half-truths. Secrecy should therefore be restricted to matters involving the good name of individuals or that touch on the rights of people whether singly or collectively.[7]

Then unfortunately shortly after John Paul II became pope

the whole *Lex* project was put to death, without explanation, in 1981 after it had been approved by a specially convened international commission earlier in the year.[8]

Nevertheless, a number of the canons of the *Lex Ecclesiae Fundamentalis* were transferred to the new 1983 Code of Canon Law and became its canons 208–223, providing a contemporary beginning of a "Catholic Constitution," but lacking a means to implement it.

NATIONAL REFORM COUNCILS

It was not only on the international level that the movement toward "participatory democracy" gained momentum in the aftermath of Vatican Council II; it also happened in a number of instances on the national level, especially in the Germanic-speaking countries and the United States, namely, in the Netherlands, West Germany, East Germany, Austria, Switzerland, and Luxemburg.[9]

The "Dutch Pastoral Council" ran in several phases from 1968 to 1979. The "West German Synod" went from 1971 to 1975; the "East German Pastoral Synod" was shorter during the same period. The "Austrian Synod" held three sessions, two in 1973 and one in 1974. The "Swiss Synod" was held in 1972, and provisions were made for subsequent national-level "Interdiocesan Pastoral Forums" from 1978 onward. The "Luxemburg Synod" was the longest running, lasting from 1972 to 1981. In almost all these instances the surveys which were stimulated and the discussions which were held were extremely responsible and progressive.

The attempt to call a National Pastoral Council in the United States got as far as a committee being set up, but no further. However, the equivalent emerged under the leadership of Cardinal John Dearden of Detroit, who spearheaded the organization of the 1976 "Call to Action," as the National Conference of Catholic Bishops' contribution to the American Bicentennial Celebration. Besides employing clerical and lay representation and majority rule voting at the 1976 assembly, the "Call to Action" stimulated widespread grass-roots consultation, including through traveling "hearings" by a committee of bishops. Finally a large number of very responsible and progressive resolutions were democratically passed at the Detroit assembly.

However, in the end, Rome was so resistant to serious democratizing developments, whether stemming from Europe or from America, that the initial general enthusiasm flowing from Vatican II progressively waned. As the French theologian Bernard Franck put it, it gave way to a

> general moroseness characteristic of the Western countries and the discouragement of a great many laity, who, here as elsewhere, watch helplessly as the church is again taken over by clergy who, as always, are jealous of their prerogatives and find it difficult to share responsibilities.[10]

This was written in 1991. Now, however, chastened progressive Catholics are beginning to strive once again for participatory democratization of the Catholic Church.

LIMITED TERM OF OFFICE

There is nothing in either Scripture or theology which necessitates an unlimited term of office for any position in the Catholic Church.

Every position, including that of pope, is "resignable"—in fact, Pope St. Celestine V resigned as pope in 1294 A.D. On the positive side, it should be noted that there are many positions which have had time limitations set to them in a variety of ways. Various positions within a diocese—for example, Vicar General, Dean, Pastor—all depend for their longevity on the will of the presiding bishop. The temporal limitation of office in these cases is known only "after the fact," not "before the fact." Bishops, and cardinals, now have a specific "before the fact" temporal limitation; namely, they must retire from their posts at age seventy-five. Further, the position of a bishop as an "Ordinary" in a particular diocese is not infrequently temporally also limited by his leaving that diocese and going to another.

There has not been a tradition of diocesan bishops being selected for their positions for a specific period of time. However, there has been the tradition for many, many centuries in the Catholic Church of the superiors of religious orders—including abbots and abbesses who often held ecclesiastical geographical jurisdiction powers comparable to those of bishops—being elected for specific limited terms of office. And all this has been duly approved by Rome.

Suffice it to recall the immense benefits of a limited term of office in the modern civil experience. The prospect of soon or at least eventually being "among" those about whom one is now making decisions is a healthy tempering thought for the decision maker. Unfettered power, with the best of will, tempts, as noted before, the realization of the famous saying of Lord Acton: "Power corrupts, and absolute power corrupts absolutely." Hence, it is no surprise that in the wake of the liberating winds of Vatican II the Catholic Theological Faculty of the University of Tübingen in Germany produced a special issue of their periodical, the *Tübinger Theologische Quartalschrift*, 2 (1969), devoted to the questions of the election and limited term of office of bishops and that the whole faculty signed a careful argument in favor of the notion of a limited term of office of eight years for resident bishops. What is perhaps surprising, however, is not that Hans Küng was one of the signers of that document (which he was) but that Joseph Ratzinger (later Cardinal and head of the Congregation for the Doctrine of the Faith, and now Pope Benedict XVI) was also![11]

SEPARATION OF POWERS

When we think of the modern democratic principle of the "separation of powers," from the time of Montesquieu's *De l'Esprit des Lois* in 1748, we normally think of the legislative, executive, and judicial powers being separated. In the ancient and medieval Catholic Church there was for long stretches of time a similar separation of powers, though the terms used were not precisely those of Montesquieu or of today. The holders of powers were: (1) bishops, (2) teachers, and in the Middle Ages (3) canon lawyers. I will deal briefly only with the first two.

It will probably come as somewhat of a shock for many Catholics to learn that in the history of the Catholic Church the pope and bishops were not always the supreme teachers of what was true Catholic doctrine. For well over nine centuries of Catholic history it was the "teachers," the theologians, who were the supreme arbiters in deciding what was correct Catholic teaching. This occurred in the first three centuries of the Christian era and again from the thirteenth through the eighteenth centuries. Concerning the first three centuries one need only remember such outstanding "teachers," who were not even priests, let alone bishops, as Clement of Alexandria (150–215 A.D.) and his successor Origen (185–254 A.D.). It is clear that there were lay teachers in the Roman Church as well in this early period for we find the Roman priest Hippolytus (170–236 A.D.) stating such in his *Apostolic Tradition:* "Whether the one who teaches be cleric or lay, he will do so."[12]

The highly regarded Cardinal Jean Daniélou clearly described the situation in the first half of the third century in Alexandria when, in writing about Origen, he stated:

> There were two distinct types of authority in the early Church. . . . The visible hierarchy of presbyters [clergy] and the visible hierarchy of doctors [free teachers]. . . . Both could be traced back to the *charismata* of the early days, but they were each derived from different ones. The two hierarchies took up different attitudes on certain points. The presbyters turned more towards the worship of God, the *didaskaloi* [free teachers] rather to the ministry of the word and to Scripture. Clearly Origen represents the viewpoint of the *didaskaloi*.[13]

It is interesting to recall that in the Gospels the term Jesus is most addressed with is not *Messiah* (Christ) or *Lord*, but *Teacher*, and the Greek of the New Testament used is *Didaskalos* (which translates the Hebrew *Rabbi*, "My Great One," "My Teacher"). In other words, Jesus was not a priest, not a bishop, he was a *Didaskalos*, a Rabbi, a Teacher, a Theologian.

Concerning the Middle Ages from the thirteenth century on no less a person than St. Thomas Aquinas clearly distinguished between the professorial chair, *cathedra magistralis*, and the episcopal throne, the *cathedra pontificalis vel pastoralis*. "The first conferred the authority to teach, *auctoritas docendi*; the second, the power to govern and, if necessary, to punish, *eminentia potestatis*."[14] There was no subordination of the magisterium of the teacher to that of the bishop; they were on an equal plane: "Teachers of sacred Scripture adhere to the ministry of the word as do also prelates."[15]

In the fourteenth century we find the French theologian Godefroid de Fontaines posing the following question (and note how he poses it): "Whether the theologian must contradict the statement of the bishop if he believes it to be opposed to the truth?" He answers that if the matter is not concerned with faith or morals, then he should dissent only in private, but if it is a matter of faith or morals,

> the teacher must take a stand, regardless of the episcopal decree ... even though some will be scandalized by this action. It is better to preserve the truth, even at the cost of a scandal than to let it be suppressed through fear of a scandal. [And, Godefroid pointed out, this would be true even if the bishop in question were the pope] for in this situation the pope can be doubted.[16]

Thus from the medieval Scholastic perspective, the theologians were supposed to determine truth and error, and it was then up to the bishops to punish the offenders. That is why from the thirteenth century onward episcopal decrees were often issued "with the counsel of teachers (*de consilio doctorum*). For example, the bishop of Paris, Etienne I, condemned several propositions as heretical "with the counsel of the teachers of theology" (*de consilio magistrorum theologiae*).[17] The Western Schism (late fourteenth and early fifteenth centuries when there were two and even three popes simultaneously!) further reinforced the prestige and authority of the theologians, so that at the two Ecumenical Councils which resolved the Western Schism, Constance (1314–18 A.D.) and especially Basel (1431–49 A.D.), there were often hundreds of theologians present and only a handful of ignorant bishops and abbots.

Hence, as Roger Gryson put it, "one cannot find any question on which the universal Church's ultimate criterion of truth did not come around to the unanimous opinion of the Scholastics [theologians], through faith in their authority (*eorum auctoritate mota*)." And by the middle of the sixteenth century the famous Spanish Dominican theologian Melchior Cano applied to theologians the words of Jesus:

> "Whoever hears you hears me, who rejects you rejects me": When the Lord said: "Who hears you hears me, and who rejects you rejects me," he did not refer with these words to the first

theologians, i.e., the apostles, but to the future teachers in the Church so long as the sheep need to be pastured in knowledge and doctrine.[18]

This "separation of powers" wherein the theologians exercised the teaching power and, as St. Thomas described it, the bishops "Regimen" or "management," continued through the end of the "Old Regimen," the French *Ancien Régime,* at the beginning of the nineteenth century.

SUBSIDIARITY

Although the concept and term "subsidiarity" was in use for many decades, it has often received short shrift in practice in the Church. Nevertheless, Pope John Paul II made some laudatory remarks about it, at least for civil society:

> Smaller social units—whether nations themselves, communities, ethnic or religious groups, families or individuals—must not be namelessly absorbed into a greater conglomeration, thus losing their identity and having their prerogatives usurped. Rather, the proper autonomy of each social class and organization, each in its own sphere, must be defended and upheld. This is nothing other than the principle of subsidiarity, which requires that a community of a higher order should not interfere in the internal life of a community of a lower order, depriving the latter of its rightful functions; instead the higher order should support the lower order and help it to coordinate its activity with that of the rest of society, always with a view to serving the common good (cf. *Centesimus Annus,* 48 [May 1, 1991]). Public opinion needs to be educated in the importance of the principle of subsidiarity. . . . (Vatican, February 23, 2000).[19]

DELIBERATION, DISSENT, DIALOGUE,
AND THEN DECISION

Question: Can there not be, indeed, ought there not be, different opinions, followed by possible dissent, then dialogue, and only thereafter decision in the Church, even on matters of the greatest religious significance? Indeed, should not this sequence of actions be adhered to *especially* in matters of the greatest religious significance?

Response: "The Christian faithful. . . . have the right and even at times a duty to manifest to the sacred pastors their opinion on matters which pertain to the good of the Church." "Those who are engaged in the sacred disciplines enjoy a lawful freedom of inquiry and of prudently expressing their opinions on matters in which they have expertise." These are not the wild words of a radical group of non-Catholics, or even of a group of liberal Catholics. They are the canons 212, 213, and 218 of the new *Code of Canon Law*. This might seem to some to seal the argument, but there is more. Recall what was cited earlier:

> Christ summons the Church, as she goes her pilgrim way, to that *continual reformation* of which she always has need. . . . Let everyone in the Church . . . preserve a proper freedom . . . even in the theological elaborations of revealed truth. . . . All are led . . . wherever necessary, to undertake with vigor *the task of renewal and reform.* . . . [All] Catholics' . . . *primary duty* is to make a careful and honest appraisal of whatever needs to be renewed and done in the Catholic household itself. [Emphasis added]

Who this time are the radical advocates of freedom and reformation "even in the theological elaborations of revealed truth"? All the Catholic bishops of the world gathered together in Ecumenical Council Vatican II (*Decree on Ecumenism*, no. 4).

Recall again that the same Council also declared that

> the human person has a right to religious freedom. This freedom means that all human beings are to be immune from coercion on the part of individuals, social groups, and every human power. . . . Nobody is forced to act against his convictions in religious matters in private or in public. . . . Truth can impose itself on the mind of humans only in virtue of its own truth. [*Declaration on Religious Liberty,* nos. 1, 2]

The Council further stated that the "search for truth" should be carried out

> by free enquiry . . . and dialogue. . . . Human beings are bound to follow their consciences faithfully in all their activity. . . . They must not be forced to act contrary to their conscience, especially in religious matters. [Ibid., no. 3]

Elsewhere the Vatican stated:

> Since the Church is a living body, she needs public opinion in order to sustain a giving and taking between her members. Without this, she cannot advance in thought and action. "Something would be lacking in her life if she had no public opinion. Both pastors of souls and lay people would be to blame for this."[20]

There is still more: In 1973 the Congregation of the Doctrine of the Faith stated that the "conceptions" by which Church teaching is expressed are changeable: "The truths which the Church intends to teach through her dogmatic formulas are distinct from the changeable conceptions of a given epoch and can be expressed without them" (Declaration *Mysterium ecclesiae*). But how can these "conceptions" be changed unless someone points out that they might be improved, might even be defective, that is, unless there is Deliberation, possibly Dissent, and then Dialogue leading to a new Decision on how to express the matter?

And a real mind boggler:

> Doctrinal discussion requires perceptiveness, both in honestly
> setting out one's own opinion and in recognizing the truth every-
> where, even if the truth demolishes one so that one is forced to
> reconsider one's own position, in theory and in practice. . . .
> Lastly, the truth will prevail by no other means than by the truth
> itself. Therefore the liberty of the participants must be ensured
> by law and reverenced in practice.[21]

Even Pope John Paul II encouraged responsible dissent and supported theologians in their invaluable service done in freedom. In
1969, then Archbishop of Kraków, he said: "Conformity means
death for any community. A loyal opposition is a necessity in any
community." A decade later, as pope, he declared that

> The Church needs her theologians, particularly in this time and
> age. . . . We desire to listen to you, and we are eager to receive the
> valued assistance of your responsible scholarship. . . . We will
> never tire of insisting on the eminent role of the university. . . . a
> place of scientific research, constantly updating its methods and
> working instruments . . . in freedom of investigation.[22]

A little later he even went so far as to remark: "Truth is the power of
peace. . . . What should one say of the practice of combatting or silenc-
ing those who do not share the same views?" (More than ironically,
even as a countersign, that statement was issued on December 18,
1979, three days after the close of the "interrogation" of Schillebeeckx
in Rome and on the very day of the quasi-silencing of Hans Küng.)

One of the main functions of the Magisterium, and especially
the Congregation of the Doctrine of the Faith, therefore, ought not
be to put a stop to **D**eliberation, **D**issent, **D**ialogue, and then **D**eci-
sion, but instead precisely to encourage, promote, and direct it in the
most creative possible channels. As a 1979 petition in support of Father Schillebeeckx signed by hundreds of theologians urged,

The function of the Congregation of the Doctrine of the Faith should be to promote dialogue among theologians of varying methodologies and approaches so that the most enlightening, helpful, and authentic expressions of theology could ultimately find acceptance. Hence, we call upon the Congregation of the Doctrine of the Faith to eliminate from its procedures "hearings," and the like, substituting for them dialogues that would be either issue-oriented, or if it is deemed important to focus on the work of a particular theologian, would bring together not only the theologian in question and the consultors of the Congregation of the Doctrine of the Faith, but also a worldwide selection of the best pertinent theological scholars of varying methodologies and approaches. These dialogues could well be conducted with the collaboration of the International Theological Commission, the Pontifical Biblical Commission, universities, theological faculties, and theological organizations. Thus, the best experts on the issues concerned would work until acceptable resolutions were arrived at. Such a procedure of course is by no means new; it is precisely the procedure utilized at the Second Vatican Council.[23]

Indeed, even the Pope and the Curia wrote of the absolute necessity of dialogue and sketched out how it should be conducted. As recalled earlier, Pope Paul VI in his first encyclical, *Ecclesiam suam* (1964), wrote that

> Dialogue is *demanded* nowadays. . . . It is *demanded* by the dynamic course of action which is changing the face of modern society. It is *demanded* by the pluralism of society and the maturity humanity has reached in this day and age. . . . This desire to impress upon the internal relationships of the Church the character of a dialogue. . . . It is, therefore, our ardent desire that the dialogue within the Church should take on new fervor, new themes and new participants, so that the holiness and vitality of the Mystical Body of Christ on earth may be increased.

Then after quoting *Ecclesiam suam* in 1968 the Vatican declared that

> the willingness to engage in dialogue is the measure and strength of that general renewal which must be carried out in the Church, which implies a still greater appreciation of liberty. . . . Doctrinal dialogue should be initiated with courage and sincerity, with the greatest freedom . . . recognizing the truth everywhere, even if the truth demolishes one so that one is forced to reconsider one's own position. . . . Therefore the liberty of the participants must be ensured by law and reverenced in practice.[24]

CONCLUSION AND CONCRETE MOVES TOWARD THE FUTURE

Thus, in summary, one can say that of course in the beginning the Church was the people, who naturally chose their leaders out of their midst; they also took an active role in deciding about a whole range of things, including doctrinal matters. It is only in the late Middle Ages and the modern period of history that the rights of the laity to choose their own Church leaders and actively to participate in Church decision-making were eroded to the tiny remnant which those of us born before Vatican II experienced growing up. We were told, however, that the way things were in our childhood was the way they had always been!

We have seen that even just before the lifetime of my great-grandparents (I was born in 1929) there flourished in two-thirds of Switzerland (the German-speaking cantons) and the southwest quarter of present-day Germany (the diocese of Constance, then the largest diocese in the world) "Enlightenment Catholicism," a "prior clone" of "Vatican II Catholicism" 150 years earlier. It was obliterated by Rome, revived at the end of the nineteenth century in so-called "Modernism," that is, "Enlightenment Catholicism

Redivivus," again crushed, only to be revived once more in "Vatican II Catholicism," that is, "Enlightenment Catholicism *Re*-Redivivus," 1962 onward.

I have argued that the major reason why the extraordinary reforms of the flourishing diocese of Constance (Enlightenment Catholicism) could be so completely obliterated, and also why its re-flourishing in so-called "Modernism" (Enlightenment Catholicism Redivivus) also could be destroyed, is that those reforms did not make it into the universal law of the Catholic Church, Canon Law. Hence, when the circumstances supporting them changed, they were mercilessly eliminated. Apparently Pope John XXIII and Pope Paul VI understood this, and therefore the former planned a thorough revision of Canon Law and the latter carried this plan forward and even set up his *Coetus* to create a Constitution. Unfortunately, the critical payment was hijacked "on the way to the bank" when Pope John Paul II dissolved the *Coetus*.

The task that Paul VI set of a Constitution for the Catholic Church must be pushed forward. Otherwise, all the advances of "Enlightenment Catholicism" "Redivivus," and "Re-Redivivus," that is, "Vatican II Catholicism," will all wash away, and our grandchildren will have to start again—if they haven't given up altogether.

How do we do this? On the international level there is the effort to promote a new Ecumenical Council in the spirit of Vatican II, which should be vigorously supported. However, it is not sufficient only to try to start from the top—and certainly not to wait for reform leadership from the top. We must *start now from below*. Every parish with a seriously responsible Pastor and core of lay leaders needs to initiate the process of gathering the parish together to discuss and write a Constitution for the parish, which it will then live by. (See appendix B for practical suggestions on how to proceed.)

What is absolutely vital, however, is that *the whole parish be deeply involved and that a* written *Constitution be produced, under which thereafter the parish will live.* Every teacher knows that open dialogue, and especially writing, produces a quality of thought that is not only precise, but also tends both to be practical and to capture the heart. A Presbyterian friend of mine once said that when he goes to important meetings, he likes to be the secretary—because what he writes, *that* is what happened at the meeting! Months and years later, what is left of all the wise words spoken in the dialogue is what was written (think of 1789 and the U.S. Supreme Court!).

Then the Parish, Pastor, leaders, and laity will live according to the Constitution that they have hammered out, adjusting it where needed as provided for in the written draft. All experience shows that the parish will be a much more dynamic, flourishing community, for it will draw on all the talents available, instead of the majority "leaving it to Beaver," and all will feel that they are both respected and nourished. When problems arise, as they inevitably do, there will be an established structure to resolve them which will assure everyone fairness. The scandals we have so often read about, or even experienced, will not have a chance to fester.

The Parish (and eventually Diocesan) Constitution also needs to be registered in law. How this is done will vary according to the area, but perhaps one simple way in the United States in general is to register the Parish as a 501(c)(3) non-profit organization with the state. This will avoid the kind of disasters a number of dioceses, and consequently parishes, found themselves in after 2002 with the myriad court cases brought because of clerical sexual abuse and subsequent episcopal cover-up.

Eventually the Pastor will leave, and the transition will be crucial, for under present Canon Law, again as Father Coriden documented above, although we all are granted rights, there is no required structure to make sure that they are respected. Hence, it is theoretically possible that an authoritarian Pastor could come in and dismiss the Constitution and practice of the previous years; however, with a mature laity who have lived a co-responsible church life for five, ten, or however many years based on its written Constitution, the Personnel Committee of the diocese and the bishop will be very reluctant to appoint a Pastor who would not work sympathetically with such a constitutional Parish.

One of the strengths of Catholicism is the tradition of giving everything important—and even things not so especially important—a liturgy. A Constitution that a parish is going to live by is in fact a *very* important sacred reality. It is a *sacramental,* and hence deserves a solemn liturgical ceremony.

The Constitution ought to be printed and framed in a fittingly solemn manner. A liturgy with an appropriate set of prayers, music, and gestures needs to be designed by the parish liturgy committee for the formal installation of the Constitution. It is important that the Pastor, the Parish Council, and other officers of the Parish, as well as as much of the entire Parish as possible, be present at the Installation liturgy. For the initial installation of the Constitution, it would be well to invite the bishop to be present as an observer (his presence will help to forestall his later sending an autocratic priest as Pastor). The Pastor, Parish Council, and other officers, as well as the rest of the Parish members present, ought to make a solemn public pledge to follow the Constitution.

An appropriate day should be chosen for the *annual* liturgical re-commitment of all to follow the Constitution—perhaps the feast day of the parish's name. Such a solemn liturgical installation, and its annual re-confirmation, will keep it present in all the parishioners' consciousness, and go a long way toward ensuring the Constitution's continuing viability.

Further, a flourishing parish which lives under its Constitution will likely inspire other Pastors and laity to do something similar in their parishes, so that it is reasonable to expect that, once started, a number of parishes over a few years will likewise go through a similar process and draft their own Constitutions (learning from their sisters' and brothers' earlier experience), and together will form a supporting network. Thus, when a Pastor from a constitutional parish leaves, a delegation from the network of "constitutional parishes" to the Personnel Committee will doubtless be very influential in determining who becomes the successor. Naturally, a time will come—hopefully sooner rather than later!—when the Pastors and people of a diocese will move to promoting the drafting of a Constitution for the diocese (there is also absolutely nothing in Canon Law inhibiting a diocesan Constitution).

Along with the critical move of casting all reforms into law—the local foundation of which is the Parish (and then the Diocesan) Constitution—is the second critical move that needs to be launched, namely, regaining financial control of church properties away from the sole control of the bishop. As was seen above, the trustee system has a very long history in the Catholic Church, but was destroyed in America through the strong-arm legal tactics of Archbishop John Hughes of New York. With three dioceses going into U.S. bankruptcy court in 2005 and the judgments coming down initially in differing directions, and more and more abuse cases pending, it is occurring to an increasing number of American Catholics, lay and clerical, that it is vital to take the church property out of the hands of the bishop alone. This critical dimension must also be reflected in the parish and diocesan Constitutions. As suggested above, perhaps a first step in that direction would be for parishes to set up 501(c)(3) non-profit organizations to be the owners of some or much of the parish properties and funds.

Again, advocating the setting up of parish and diocesan councils with Constitutions is not some wild *novum*. The representatives of all the bishops of the world gathered together in Rome in 1971 at its International Synod of Bishops supported such:

> The members of the Church should have some share in the drawing up of decisions, in accordance with the rules given by the Second Vatican Ecumenical Council and the Holy See, for instance with regard to the setting up of councils at all levels.[25]

Then the pressure from below will mount for a new Global Constitutional Convention and we (or likely our descendants) will be able to celebrate the ratification of the greatest single advance in Catholicism in centuries—a *Catholic Constitution* for reform and renewal, a constitution called for by Pope Paul VI, revised by the People of God, and established incrementally in our local, provincial, national, and regional communities. We will then have a Church *of* the People of God, *by* the People of God, and *for* the People of God! AMEN!

NOTES

1. Cf. Pope John Paul II, *Apostolic Constitution Sacrae disciplinae leges*, in *Code of Canon Law. Latin-English Edition* (Washington, D.C.: Canon Law Society of America, 1983), p. ix.

2. James A. Coriden, "A Challenge: Making the Rights Real," in Leonard Swidler and Herbert O'Brien (a pseudonym for protective purposes), *A Catholic Bill of Rights* (Kansas City: Sheed & Ward, 1988), p. 11; also in *The Jurist*, 45, 1 (1985).

3. *Textus Emendatus*, Vatican Press, pp. 119–20, 123, cited in Peter Hebblethwaite, *Pope Paul VI* (New York: Paulist Press, 1993), p. 573.

4. Coriden, "A Challenge," p. 11.

5. *Communicationes* 1 (1969), pp. 77–100. *Patribus synodi episcoporum habenda* (Vatican: Typis Polyglottis Vaticanis, 1969), pp. 80, 79.

6. Report by Peter Nichols in *The Times* (London), July 6, 1971.

7. *Communio et progressio*, published in Austin Flannery, ed., *Vatican Council II* (Collegeville, Minn.: Liturgical Press, 1975), p. 332.

8. Coriden, "A Challenge," p. 11.

9. For information on the "national" synods in the Germanic-speaking countries see the detailed essay by the priest and theologian Bernard Franck, "Experiences of National Synods in Europe After the Council," in James Provost and Knut Walf, eds., *The Tabu of Democracy within the Church, Concilium*, 1992/5 (London: SCM Press, 1992), pp. 82–97. For further analysis of the West German Synod and its aftermath, as well as the U.S. equivalent, the 1976 "Call to Action," see Heinrich Fries, *Suffering From the Church*, introduction and translation by Leonard and Arlene Swidler (Collegeville, Minn.: Liturgical Press, 1994).

10. Franck, "National Synods," p. 92.

11. See the expanded English translation, Leonard Swidler and Arlene Swidler, eds. and trans., *Bishops and People* (Philadelphia: Westminster Press, 1970).

12. *Apostolic Tradition* (Hippolytus), XIX.

13. Jean Daniélou, *Origen* (New York: 1955), p. 50.

14. Roger Gryson, "The Authority of the Teacher in the Ancient and Medieval Church," in Leonard Swidler and Piet Fransen, eds. *Authority in the Church and the Schillebeeckx Case* (New York: Crossroad, 1982), p. 184.

15. Thomas Aquinas, *Quodlibitales*, III, a. 9. "Doctores sacrae scripturae adhibentur ministerio verbi Dei, sicut et praelati."

16. References and fuller discussion in Gryson, "The Authority of the Teacher," pp. 176–87.

17. Ibid., p. 186.

18. Citation found in ibid., pp. 186ff. The original reads: "Cum Dominus dixit: Qui vos audit me audit, et qui vos spernit me spernit, non modo ad primos theologos, i.e. apostolos verba illa referebat, sed ad doctores etiam in Ecclesia futuros, quamdiu pascendae essent oves in scientia et doctrina."

19. "Message of the Holy Father John Paul II to the Participants in the Sixth Plenary Session of the Pontifical Academy of Social Sciences" (http://www.vatican.va/holy_father/john_paul_ii/speeches/2000/jan-mar/documents/hf _jpii_spe_20000223_acdsciencesplenary_en.html).

20. Following up on Vatican II's *Decree on the Pastoral Means of Social Communication*, the Vatican's Pontifical Council for the Instruments of Social Communication issued in 1971 its "Pastoral Instruction on the Means of Social Instruction" (*Communio et progressio*) found in Flannery, *Vatican Council II*, p. 330. Its internal quotation is of Pope Pius XII: Allocution given on 17 February 1950 to those who were in Rome to participate in the International Congress for Editors of Catholic Periodicals, *AAS* 42 (1950), p. 25.

21. Words of the Vatican Curia (!) in 1968: Vatican Secretariat for Unbelievers, *Humanae personae dignitatem*, in Flannery, *Vatican Council II*, p. 1,010.

22. "Address to Catholic Theologians and Scholars at the Catholic University of America," October 7, 1979, emphasis added.

23. Reprinted in Leonard Swidler, *Küng in Conflict* (New York: Doubleday, 1981), pp. 516 ff.

24. *Humanae personae dignitatem*, quoted in Flannery, *Vatican Council II*, pp. 1,003, 1,007, 1,010 (emphasis added).

25. Reprinted in part in the *Charter of the Rights of Catholics in the Church* of the Association for the Rights of Catholics in the Church (ARCC), 2nd ed., January 1985, p. 17.

A Proposed Constitution of the Catholic Church

*T*his Constitution provides the framework within which the Catholic Church governs itself. The Constitution sets forth the fundamental rights and corresponding responsibilities of members and the basic structure for decision making and action within the Catholic Church. All laws, regulations, and customs of the Catholic Church shall be carried out within this Constitution's framework and spirit.

I. PREAMBLE

1. We the people of the Catholic Church hold that because all men and women are created in God's image and likeness and that the same divine teaching on how they should live is written in every human heart, all persons are to be treated with dignity and equality, each person having the same fundamental rights and responsibilities.

2. We hold that by our faith in God through Jesus and our baptism with water and the Holy Spirit, all Christians become "members of the body of Christ," that is, the Church universal, and are committed to living out the Gospel proclaimed and lived by Jesus. We further hold that all Christians who recognize the Ministry of

139

Unity which has historically been exercised by the Bishop of Rome, are members of the Catholic Church (hereafter, simply, the Church).

3. We hold that the Church's mission, grounded in the Gospel, is to proclaim and show forth Jesus' Good News of how to live a fully human life as images of God in individual and communal justice and love. We hold that the Church realizes this mission within the context of the laws which it enacts to foster and preserve the spirit of the Gospel and to assist its members as they endeavor to live in the love of God and neighbor.

Fundamental to the Church's mission are certain rights and responsibilities which pertain to all members.

II. RIGHTS AND RESPONSIBILITIES

The following are the Church members' fundamental rights, flowing either from their basic human rights or their basic baptismal rights. Each right entails a corresponding responsibility on the part of the rights holders, some of which are so obvious that they do not require specific articulation. In all instances these rights and responsibilities apply to all Catholics, regardless of race, age, nationality, sex, sexual orientation, state-of-life, or social or economic position.

A. Basic Human Rights and Responsibilities

1. All Catholics have the basic human rights—e.g., (a) freedom of action, (b) freedom of conscience, (c) freedom of opinion and expression, (d) the right to receive and impart information, (e) freedom of association, (f) the right to due process of law, (g) the right of participation in self-governance, (h) the right to the accountability of chosen leaders, (i) the right to the safeguarding of one's reputation and privacy, (j) the right to marry, (k) the

right to education—and the corresponding duty to exercise them responsibly.

2. As a consequence of the basic human right of freedom of action, all Catholics have the right to engage in any activity which neither causes harm nor infringes on the rights of others.

3. As a consequence of the basic human right of freedom of conscience, all Catholics have the right and responsibility to follow their informed consciences in all matters.

4. As a consequence of the basic human right to receive and impart information, all Catholics have the right of access to all information possessed by Church authorities concerning their own spiritual and temporal welfare, provided such access does not infringe on the rights of others.

5. As a consequence of the basic human right of freedom of opinion and expression, all Catholics have the right to express publicly in a responsible manner their agreement or disagreement regarding decisions made by Church authorities.

   a) Laity have the right and responsibility to make their opinions known in a responsible manner, especially where they have first-hand experience of the issue at hand.

   b) Catholic teachers and scholars of theology have a right to, and responsibility for, academic freedom; the acceptability of their teaching is to be judged in dialogue with their peers—and, when appropriate, Church authorities. Such scholars and teachers will keep in mind that the search for truth and its expression entails following wherever the evidence leads, and hence, the legitimacy of responsible dissent and pluralism of thought and its expression.

6. As a consequence of the basic human right of freedom of association, all Catholics have the right to form voluntary associations to pursue Catholic aims; such associations have the right to decide on their own rules of governance.

7. As a consequence of the basic human right to due process of law, all Catholics have the right to be dealt with according to

commonly accepted norms of fair administrative and judicial procedures without undue delay, and to redress of grievances through regular procedures of law.

8. As a consequence of the basic human right of participation in self-governance, all Catholics have the right to a voice in decisions that affect them, including the choosing of their leaders, and a duty to exercise those rights responsibly.

9. As a consequence of the basic human right to the accountability of chosen leaders, all Catholics have the right to have their leaders render an account to them.

10. As a consequence of the basic human right to the safeguarding of one's reputation and privacy, all Catholics have the right not to have their good reputations impugned or their privacy violated.

11. As a consequence of the basic human right to marry, all Catholics have the right to choose their state in life; this includes the right for both laity and clergy to marry, remain single, or embrace celibacy.

12. As a consequence of the basic human right to marry, with each spouse retaining full and equal rights during marriage, all Catholics have the right to withdraw from a marriage which has irretrievably broken down.

    a) All such Catholics retain the radical right to remarry; and

    b) All divorced and remarried Catholics who are in conscience reconciled to the Church retain the right to the same ministries, including all the sacraments, as do other Catholics.

13. As a consequence of the basic human rights to marry and to education, all Catholic parents have the right and responsibility

    a) To determine in conscience the size of their families,

    b) To choose appropriate methods of family planning, and

    c) To see to the education of their children.

B. Basic Baptismal Rights and Responsibilities

1. As a consequence of their baptism, all Catholics have the right to receive in the Church those ministries which are needed for the living of a fully Christian life, including:

   a) Worship which reflects the joys and concerns of the gathered community and instructs and inspires it;

   b) Instruction in the Christian tradition and the presentation of spirituality and moral teaching in a way that promotes the helpfulness and relevance of Christian values to contemporary life; and

   c) Pastoral care that applies with concern and effectiveness the Christian heritage to persons in particular situations.

2. As a consequence of baptism, all Catholics have the right

   a) To receive all the sacraments for which they are adequately prepared; and

   b) To exercise all ministries in the Church for which they are adequately prepared, according to the needs and with the approval or commissioning of the community.

3. As a consequence of their baptism, all Catholics have the right to expect that the resources of the Church expended within the Church will be fairly distributed on their behalf. Among other concerns, this implies that

   a) All Catholic women have an equal right with men to the resources and the exercise of all the powers of the Church;

   b) All Catholic parents have the right to expect fair material and other assistance from Church leaders in the religious education of their children; and

   c) All single Catholics have the right to expect that the resources of the Church be fairly expended on their behalf.

4. As a consequence of their baptism, as well as the social nature of humanity, all Catholics have the corresponding responsibility to support the Church through their time, talents and financial resources.

III. GOVERNANCE STRUCTURES

A. Fundamental Insights

1. Through the centuries the Church has wrestled with the concrete issues of the exercise of power and law, without which no society can survive, let alone develop humanly. In this long period the Church both benefited and suffered from many experiments with power and law in a great variety of cultures. In testing them for itself the Church gained wisdom in both negative and positive ways, i.e., it learned much about what works well and what does not.

2. Two key insights gained from all these experiences are fundamental for the governance of the Church in the third millennium. One is that shared responsibility and corresponding freedom are at the heart of being human, both individually and communally. The second is that the most effective means of arriving at an ever fuller understanding of reality is through dialogue, which should be carried on both within the Church and with those outside the Church. It is on this long experience and wisdom of the Church, especially these two key insights, that this Constitution draws and builds in its governance structures.

B. Principles

1. It is of the essence of the Church to be a community. The most basic unit of that Church community is where members daily live their lives, beginning with the family and other intimate associations. Beyond this the fundamental unit of the Church is a local community, most often but not exclusively the geographical parish.

2. It is, however, also of the essence of the Church that it is a communion of communities, so that the local communities are also united in intermediate-level communities, most often but not ex-

clusively the geographical diocese, and they in turn in national communities, and these finally in the global community of the universal Catholic Church. In addition, other communions of church communities, such as regional or multinational communions, may be developed as warranted, based on geography, language, or other factors.

3. In keeping with the spirit of the Gospel, developing human experience, and the dynamic Christian tradition, especially its two key insights of shared responsibility–corresponding freedom and dialogue, the following basic principles shall shape the governing structures and regulations of the Church:

   a) The principle of subsidiarity shall rule throughout the Church, that is, all decision-making rights and responsibilities shall remain with the smaller community unless the good of the broader community specifically demands that it exercise those rights and responsibilities.

   b) Throughout the Church the formulations and applications of the tradition shall be arrived at through a process of charitable and respectful dialogue.

   c) Throughout the Church each community shall form its own body of governing regulations.

   d) Throughout the Church leaders shall be elected to office through appropriate structures, giving voice to all respective constituents.

   e) Leaders shall hold office for a specified, limited term.

   f) A separation of legislative, executive and judicial powers, along with a system of checks and balances, shall be observed. This entails representatively elected councils and leaders, as well as established judicial systems at all levels. All branches share responsibility in ways appropriate to the spirit of the Gospel and this Constitution.

   g) All leaders and councils will regularly provide their constituents an account of their work, including financial accounts, to be reviewed by an outside auditor when appropriate.

h) All groupings of the faithful, including women and minorities, shall be equitably represented in all positions of leadership and decision making.

C. *Councils*

1. At every level of church communion—local, diocesan, national, and universal, or other as warranted—representative councils shall be established which shall serve as the principal decision-making bodies. Each council is to observe the following:
   a) The principles of subsidiarity and dialogue are to characterize the deliberations and decisions of each council.
   b) Members of the councils shall be elected in as representative a manner as possible, including, when appropriate, representatives of various organizations within that church.
   c) Members of councils shall serve for a specified term of office. Councils at each level shall formulate their own body of governing regulations, bearing in mind the appropriate regulations of the broader communities.
   d) Each council's governing regulations shall determine the number, manner of election, and term of office of members, how the chair is chosen, and how decision-making responsibilities are to be distributed, as well as specifying other church procedures, preserving the basic governance principles expressed in this Constitution.
   e) The rule of one person, one vote shall prevail in all councils.
   d) At the national, multinational and universal levels, councils shall include among their members at least 30% commissioned office holders of ministries and 30% other faithful.
   f) No one shall have veto power.
   i) Local Church
1. The members of every Parish (or equivalent) shall elect a Council, which shall be the principal decision-making body of the Parish. The Pastor shall be an ex officio member of the Council.

2. If there is not already a parish body of governing regulations, the Parish Council shall formulate such, to be approved by the Parish, bearing in mind the appropriate regulations of the regional and broader communities.

3. The Parish Council, either directly or through committees, shall bear ultimate responsibility for Parish policy on worship, education, social outreach, administration, finances and other activities carried out in the name of the Parish.

ii) Diocesan Church

1. Every Diocese shall elect a Diocesan Council, which shall be the principal decision-making body of the Diocese. The Bishop of the Diocese is ex officio a member of the Council, which shall be composed of at least 30% commissioned office holders of ministries and 30% other faithful.

2. If there is not already a Diocesan Constitution and/or body of governing regulations, the Diocesan Council shall formulate one or both, to be approved by two-thirds of the Parish Councils of the Diocese, bearing in mind the appropriate regulations of the national and international communities.

3. The Diocesan Council, either directly or through committees or agencies, shall bear ultimate responsibility for diocesan policy and regulations on worship, education, social outreach, administration, finances and other activities carried out in the name of the Diocese.

iii) National Church

1. Normally the Diocesan Councils of a nation will establish a National Council. If for reasons of size or other constraints certain Diocesan Councils decide that establishing a National Council would not be appropriate for them, they shall apply to the General Council for permission to join or establish an appropriate alternative superior Council. The National Council, or its alternative, shall be the principal decision-making body of the National Church. A bishop and a layperson elected by the National Council shall be Co-Chairs of the National Council, which shall be

composed of at least 30% commissioned office holders of ministries and 30% other faithful.

2. If there is not already a National Constitution and/or body of governing regulations, the National Council shall formulate one or both, to be approved by two-thirds of the Diocesan Councils of the nation, bearing in mind the appropriate regulations of the Universal Church and this Constitution.

3. The National Council, either directly or through committees or agencies, shall bear ultimate responsibility for national policy and regulations on worship, education, social outreach, administration, finances and other activities carried out in the name of the National Council.

iv) Multinational Church

1. If several National Councils (e.g., of a continent or discrete geographical area, etc.) decide it would be helpful to gather formally, they will formulate a multinational body of regulations by which to govern themselves, to be approved by two-thirds of the National Councils involved, bearing in mind the appropriate regulations of the Universal Church and this Constitution.

v) Universal Church

1. The National Councils shall every ten years elect a General Council, which shall function as the principal decision-making body of the Universal Church. The General Council shall bear ultimate responsibility for the formulation of the laws and regulations governing the Universal Church as well as the establishment of policies and regulations concerning doctrine, morals, worship, education, social outreach, administration, finances, and other activities carried out in the name of the Universal Church, bearing especially in mind the principle of subsidiarity. The Pope and a layperson elected by the General Council shall be Co-Chairs of the General Council.

2. The members of the General Council, being a total of 500, shall be elected in staggered fashion for ten-year terms. The General Council shall meet at least once a year.

3. The General Council is composed of 500 delegates chosen by the National Councils proportional to the number of registered Catholics in the countries concerned. Countries with a smaller number of Catholics than required for at least one delegate shall join together into larger units.

4. If there is not already a General Council Constitution and/or body of governing regulations, the first General Council shall formulate one or both, to be approved by two-thirds of the National Councils, preserving the basic governance principles expressed in this Constitution.

5. The Constitution of the General Council and its governing regulations, together with the governing regulations of all the offices which it shall set up, shall all have the same legal status as the Constitution. Any amendments to the aforementioned shall be subject to the section V Amendments procedures of this Constitution.

6. The General Council shall set up within its first year the Papal Election Commission. Any amendments to the Constitution and governing regulations of the Papal Election Commission shall be subject to the section V Amendments procedures of this Constitution. The Papal Election Commission shall be independent of the General Council.

7. The General Council shall through committees or agencies bear ultimate responsibility for implementing the laws, regulations and policies of the Universal Church.

D. Leaders

i) General

1. All leaders, including commissioned holders of ministries, shall be appropriately trained and experienced.

2. Commissioned holders of ministries are church leaders who normally work full-time for the church and are chosen by the appropriate church community to act in its name.

3. All commissioned holders of ministries shall be chosen in a manner which shall give a representative voice to all those who are to be led by them. This is especially true of the local Pastor, the Diocesan Bishop, and the Pope.

4. All commissioned holders of ministries shall serve for specified terms of office. The Diocesan Constitution shall specify the term and renewability of office of the Pastor. The National Constitution shall specify the term and renewability of office of the Diocesan Bishop.

5. All commissioned holders of ministries can be removed from office only for cause, following a procedure of due process based on principles enunciated in this Constitution.

6. All commissioned holders of ministries have responsibilities and corresponding rights which must be specified by the respective Constitutions; those of Pastor, Bishop, and Pope are especially laid out here.

   ii) Pastor

1. Pastors shall be chosen by the parish (or its equivalent) and approved by the Bishop and the Diocesan Council in accordance with the procedures set forth in the Diocesan Constitution.

2. The Pastor shall serve as the leader of the Parish pastoral team. Within the policies set by the Parish Council, they bear the main responsibility for the worship, spiritual and moral instruction, and pastoral care dimensions of the Parish. This responsibility entails:

   a) Worship that reflects the joys and concerns of the gathered community and instructs and inspires it;

   b) Instruction in the Christian tradition and the presentation of spirituality and moral teaching in a way that promotes the helpfulness and relevance of Christian values to contemporary life; and

   c) Pastoral care that applies with love and effectiveness the Christian heritage to persons in particular situations.

3. Pastors have both a right to and responsibility for proper training and continuation of their education throughout the term of their office.

4. Pastors have a right to fair financial support for the exercise of their office, as well as the requisite liberty needed for the proper exercise thereof.

   iii) Bishop

1. The Bishop shall be chosen by the Diocesan Council in accordance with the Diocesan Constitution, bearing in mind the appropriate regulations of the national and international communities, including consultation with and subsequent confirmation by the appropriate committees of the National Council and General Council.

2. The Bishop shall serve as the leader of the Diocesan pastoral team. Within the policies set by the Diocesan Council, they bear the main responsibility for the worship, spiritual and moral instruction, and pastoral care dimensions of the Diocese, bearing in mind the principle of subsidiarity.

   iv) Pope

1. The Pope of the Universal Church shall be elected for a single ten-year term by Delegates selected by the National Councils.

   a) The number of Delegates from National Councils to the Papal Election Congress shall be proportional to the number of registered Catholics in a nation, to be determined by an appropriate international committee.

   b) The Delegates shall be chosen as representatively as possible, one-third being bishops.

2. The Pope together with the General Council and their agencies and committees bears the main responsibility for carrying out the policies set by the General Council, especially in the areas of the worship, doctrinal, moral and spiritual instruction, and pastoral care functions of the Universal Church, bearing in mind the principle of subsidiarity.

IV. JUDICIAL SYSTEM

A. *Principles*

1. The Catholic Church is a pilgrim church, always in need of reform and correction. Disputes, contentions, and crimes against the rights of members will regrettably occur. These are to be resolved by processes of conciliation and arbitration. Where this proves impossible, Catholics may take such cases to the Church's tribunals for adjudication. All Catholics are entitled to fair and due process under ecclesiastical law. All personnel involved in the Church's judicial system shall be appropriately trained and competent.
2. A system of diocesan, provincial, national and international tribunals shall be established, which shall serve as courts of first instance, each with designated courts of appeal. These tribunals shall be governed by this Constitution and subsequent laws in keeping with it.

B. *Tribunals*

i) *Local and Regional*

1. Every diocese shall establish a tribunal, or make other arrangements, for the judicial hearing of contentious and criminal cases which are brought before it by its people.
   a) Diocesan tribunals shall have competence over all matters which pertain to the internal order of the local and regional Church. These include all acts defined by the general ecclesiastical law as administrative acts, crimes, jurisdictional disputes, and matters of equity and restitution.
   b) Diocesan tribunals shall conduct their operations according to the procedural law established by the Universal Church.

    c) Appeals against the judgment of the diocesan tribunal shall be heard by the tribunal of the respective ecclesiastical province.

2. All cases involving a Diocesan Bishop shall be heard by the national tribunal.

ii) National

1. The National Council shall establish where appropriate provincial appellate courts and an appellate tribunal which shall serve as court of second instance for all cases, judicial or administrative, which are brought before it by its provincial tribunals.

2. Appeals from the decisions of this tribunal shall be heard by the Supreme Tribunal.

iii) International

1. Where there are no National Tribunals the General Council shall establish where appropriate multinational appellate tribunals which shall serve as courts of second instance.

2. The General Council shall establish a Supreme Tribunal which shall serve as the court of final appeal for all cases brought before it by lower courts or by the General Council.

3. The Supreme Tribunal shall hear cases charging illegal or unconstitutional actions by the Pope.

4. There shall be no judicial appeal from the judgments of the Supreme Tribunal.

C. Continued Fitness for Office of Leaders

Church leaders shall serve out their elected term of office unless the question of competence and continued fitness for office is formally raised in accordance with constitutionally established norms. Determination of such competence and fitness for office may be made by the office-holder's ecclesiastical superior or by the appropriate Council, due process being observed. In the case of the Pope, such determination is to be made by a regular or special session of the General Council.

V. AMENDMENTS

This Constitution can be amended by a three-quarters vote of the General Council, and a subsequent ratification by three-fourths of the National Councils within a five-year period after the passage of the amendment by the General Council.

VI. IMPLEMENTATION

This Constitution will come into force upon its adoption by a duly authorized Constitutional Convention.
September 19, 1998, Version
Association for the Rights of Catholics in the Church (ARCC)
http://arcc-catholic-rights.org/

· *Appendix B* ·

Parish (Diocesan) Constitution: Procedural Guidelines

I. GOALS

This is what a Parish (or Diocesan) *Constitution* (or *Covenant*) should have when fully developed. They may not be immediately obtainable, but for progress it is vital to have a vision of these goals; only then can strategies to reach them be developed. *Reminder:* It is absolutely *essential* that the parish *write* a Constitution, and then *live* by it.

A. Decision-Making Power

All aspects of parish life should be under the jurisdiction of the Constitution, which in subsidiarity will be in line with the Constitutions of higher bodies; any action contrary to it would be void. The rights and responsibilities of all parish officers and agencies should be clearly spelled out. Lay women and men as well as clergy should have real decision-making power—not merely advisory.

B. Representativeness

All bodies of the parish, especially the Parish Council, should be equitably representative, being chosen from the entire community, including all elements, e.g., women, men, young, old, single, married.

C. A Bill of Rights

The rights of all individuals and groups must be spelled out clearly in a Bill of Rights–Responsibilities section.

D. Due Process of Law

There needs to be a judicial body which can adjudicate all complaints and protect the rights of all as listed in the Constitution; it needs to have real decision-making power to which everyone is subject.

E. Accountability/Transparency

All decision-making must be accountable to its responsible superior and eventually the whole parish. With appropriate safeguards for personal privacy, all decision-making must be transparent to all.

II. INTERIM STEPS

A. Start Where You Are

"Rome was not built in a day"—nor was it transformed in one either! Remember, the best can be the enemy of the good. Start wherever you are in your parish by using the possibilities that are actually present. *You* get involved in your parish by volunteering, accepting a responsibility. Make yourself, and like-minded "democracy-oriented" parishioners, accepted so your opinion will carry more weight. *Note:* Canons 537 and 1280 require Finance Committees with decision-making power.

B. Dialogue

If you don't already have a perfect parish with a perfectly functioning Constitution—and fellow parishioners are not going to immediately fall in line when you suggest that you ought to have a fully democratic parish with a Constitution—perhaps they will need to be persuaded. You too will have much to learn from them and together with them. The way to make all this happen is through dialogue, meaning first of all respectful, open listening, and then clear, respectful explaining of your ideas. As the ancient Latin phrase has it: *Festine lente!* Make haste slowly!

C. Education to Change Catholic Consciousness to Become Pro-Democracy/Constitution

Many Catholics will be very suspicious, or even worse, of the idea of a democratic Catholicism and of a Constitution. Many will have the "feeling" that such "politics" does not belong in a sacred body like the Church. In the wake of all the sexual abuse scandals, this is beginning to change, and the momentum should be seized upon. Perhaps the most important thing that needs to be done in order to usher in a more democratic Catholicism and a Constitution is changing Catholic consciousness to accept and affirm them. This will require a massive education program through books, articles, lectures, study groups, field visits, etc.

D. Making All Accountable and Transparent

In the wake of the national clerical sexual abuse scandals, it is imperative that all decision making be completely transparent. This is especially important in financial matters. Use whatever bodies are available to urge transparency and accountability—personal conversations, public statements at meetings of all parish bodies, letters, parish bulletin, etc.

III. LITURGICAL INSTALLATION OF THE PARISH CONSTITUTION

One of the strengths of Catholicism is the tradition of giving every thing important—and even things not so especially important—a liturgy. A *Constitution* that a parish is going to live by is in fact a *very* important sacred reality. It is a *sacramental,* and hence deserves a solemn liturgical ceremony.

After the *Constitution* has been carefully discussed and drafted with the active participation of all elements of the Parish, it ought to be printed and framed in a fittingly solemn manner. A liturgy with an appropriate set of prayers, music, and gestures needs to be designed by the parish liturgy committee for the formal installation of the *Constitution.* It is important that the Pastor, the Parish Council, and other officers of the Parish, as well as as much of the entire Parish as possible, be present at the Installation liturgy. For the initial installation of the *Constitution,* it would be well to invite the bishop to be present as an observer (his presence will help to forestall his later sending an autocratic priest as Pastor). The Pastor, Parish Council, and other officers, as well as the rest of the Parish members present, ought to make a solemn public pledge to follow the *Constitution.*

An appropriate day should be chosen for the *annual* liturgical re-commitment of all to follow the *Constitution*—perhaps the feast day of the parish's name.

Such a solemn liturgical installation, and its annual re-confirmation, will keep it present in all the parishioners' consciousness, and go a long way toward ensuring the *Constitution's* continuing viability.

Association for the Rights of Catholics in the Church (ARCC)
http://arcc-catholic-rights.org/

Index

About the Author

Leonard Swidler is professor of Catholic thought and interreligious dialogue at Temple University in Philadelphia. With his wife Arlene Anderson Swidler, he is the editor of the *Journal of Ecumenical Studies*. He is also the founder and director of the Institute for Interreligious and Intercultural Dialogue.